# Charles Tomlinson

SELECTED POEMS / 1955-1997

## Poetry by Charles Tomlinson

Annunciations

The Door in the Wall

The Flood

Jubilation

The Return

Seeing Is Believing

Selected Poems

# Charles Tomlinson

## SELECTED POEMS / 1955-1997

A NEW DIRECTIONS BOOK

Manufactured in the United States of America
New Directions books are printed on acid-free paper.
First published as New Directions Paperbook 855 in 1997
Published simultaneously in Canada by Penguin Books Canada

Published by arrangement with Oxford University Press.

Library of Congress Cataloging-in-Publication Data

Tomlinson, Charles, 1927-
[Poems. Selections]
Selected poems, 1955-1997 / Charles Tomlinson.
p.    cm.
ISBN 0-8112-1369-2 (acid-free paper)
I. Title
OR6039.0349A6                                        1997
821'.914—dc21                                        97-25373
                                                          CIP

New Directions Books are published for James Laughlin
by New Directions Publishing Corporation,
80 Eighth Avenue, New York 10011

*To Brenda*

xi

# PREFACE

These poems were written between my mid-twenties and my seventieth year. Most of the early volume, *The Necklace*, was the result of a period of employment (1951–2) in Italy. That country, which confirmed me in my vocation as a poet as soon as I saw its light falling on the Bay of Lerici, has been a place to which the poems frequently return. My other literary and geographic debt is to America—to its poetry and to the deserts of New Mexico and the spaces of upstate New York. These contrasting geographies, both topographical and poetic, gave me a vantage from which to experience afresh my heritage as an Englishman and a European. The present volume does not contain any of my translations, but the effect of other poetries—French, German, Italian and Spanish— was also to challenge and suggest new possibilities for my own, and also to revivify my sense of that long continuity going back to Chaucer, *le grant translateur*, who brought our island traditions closer to French and Italian.

When I began writing poems we were at war and Europe was in chaos. Poetry inevitably became an instrument of restoration and a reaching out to the heritage we seemed about to lose. Two men, Cecil Scrimgeour, a Scot with strong French affiliations, and Gerhardt Kuttner, a refugee from Hitler's Germany, were the first to awaken me to all that lay out there and belonged to us young linguists in a grammar school in the English midlands. What better beginnings could a youthful poet from a non-literary background have asked for? My first 'real' poem was unmistakably English— I had never left this island at the time of writing it—, but the invitation of space in it would infallibly lead to an involvement with both foreign places and with world literature—the *Weltliteratur* one of my two mentors had constantly spoken of:

> Wakening with the window over fields
> To the coin-clear harness-jingle as a float
> Clips by, and each succeeding hoof fall, now remote,
> Breaks clean and frost-sharp on the unstopped ear.

The hooves describe an arabesque on space,
A dotted line in sound that falls and rises
As the cart goes by, recedes, turns to retrace
Its way back through the unawakened village.

And space vibrates, enlarges with the sound;
Though space is soundless, yet creates
From very soundlessness a ground
To counterstress the lilting hoof fall as it breaks.

In this poem, coming from a far-off era when milk was delivered in a float, English and American sources were unexpectedly combined: 'the unstopped ear' is a phrase from Pound's *Hugh Selwyn Mauberley* where Ulysses, bound to the mast, has refused to have his ears stopped with wax, so that he can listen to the song of the sirens in all its challenging strangeness. Pound somehow became entangled for me with Hopkins whose thrush 'does so rinse and wring / The ear . . .' Playing with a stressed metre akin to Hopkins', I felt my own ear was gradually unstopping. When I say this was my first 'real' poem, I mean that from then on I heard a new music entering my poetry—not the song of the sirens, but the song of a universe that offered an otherness that was both concrete and inexhaustible.

C.T. 1997

# Charles Tomlinson

SELECTED POEMS / 1955-1997

# *The Necklace* (1955)

## AESTHETIC

Reality is to be sought, not in concrete,
But in space made articulate:
The shore, for instance,
Spreading between wall and wall;
The sea-voice
Tearing the silence from the silence.


## VENICE

Cut into by doors
The morning assumes night's burden,
The houses assemble in tight cubes.

From the palace flanking the waterfront
She is about to embark, but pauses.
Her dress is a veil of sound
Extended upon silence.

Under the bridge,
Contained by the reflected arc
A tunnel of light
Effaces walls, water, horizon.

Floating upon its own image
A cortège of boats idles through space.

# NINE VARIATIONS IN A
# CHINESE WINTER SETTING

### I

Warm flute on the cold snow
Lays amber in sound.

### II

Against brushed cymbal
Grounds yellow on green,
Amber on tinkling ice.

### III

The sage beneath the waterfall
Numbers the blessing of a flute;
Water lets down
Exploding silk.

### IV

The hiss of raffia,
The thin string scraped with the back of the bow
Are not more bat-like
Than the gusty bamboos
Against a flute.

### V

Pine-scent
In snow-clearness
Is not more exactly counterpointed
Than the creak of trodden snow
Against a flute.

### VI

The outline of the water-dragon
Is not embroidered with so intricate a thread
As that with which the flute
Defines the tangible borders of a mood.

### VII

The flute in summer makes streams of ice:
In winter it grows hospitable.

### VIII

In mist, also, a flute is cold
Beside a flute in snow.

### IX

Degrees of comparison
Go with differing conditions:
Sunlight mellows lichens,
Whereas snow mellows the flute.


## SEA CHANGE

To define the sea —
We change our opinions
With the changing light.

Light struggles with colour:
A quincunx
Of five stones, a white
Opal threatened by emeralds.

The sea is uneasy marble.

The sea is green silk.

The sea is blue mud, churned
By the insistence of wind.

Beneath dawn a sardonyx may be cut from it
In white layers laced with a carnelian orange,
A leek- or apple-green chalcedony
Hewn in the cold light.

Illustration is white wine
Floating in a saucer of ground glass
On a pedestal of cut glass:

A static instance, therefore untrue.


## FIASCHERINO


Over an ash-fawn beach fronting a sea which keeps
    Rolling and unrolling, lifting
The green fringes from submerged rocks
    On its way in, and, on its way out
Dropping them again, the light

Squanders itself, a saffron morning
    Advances among foam and stones, sticks
Clotted with black naphtha
    And frayed to the newly carved
Fresh white of chicken flesh.

One leans from the cliff-top. Height
    Distances like an inverted glass; the shore
Is diminished but concentrated, jewelled
    With the clarity of warm colours
That, seen more nearly, would dissipate

Into masses. The map-like interplay
    Of sea-light against shadow
And the mottled close-up of wet rocks
    Drying themselves in the hot air
Are lost to us. Content with our portion,

Where, we ask ourselves, is the end of all this
    Variety that follows us? Glare
Pierces muslin; its broken rays
    Hovering in trembling filaments
Glance on the ceiling with no more substance

Than a bee's wing. Thickening, these
    Hang down over the pink walls
In green bars, and, flickering between them,
    A moving fan of two colours,
The sea unrolls and rolls itself into the low room.

## THE ATLANTIC

Launched into an opposing wind, hangs
   Grappled beneath the onrush,
And there, lifts, curling in spume,
   Unlocks, drops from that hold
Over and shoreward. The beach receives it,
   A whitening line, collapsing
Powdering-off down its broken length;
   Then, curded, shallow, heavy
With clustering bubbles, it nears
   In a slow sheet that must climb
Relinquishing its power, upward
   Across tilted sand. Unravelled now
And the shore, under its lucid pane,
   Clear to the sight, it is spent:
The sun rocks there, as the netted ripple
   Into whose skeins the motion threads it
Glances athwart a bed, honey-combed
   By heaving stones. Neither survives the instant
But is caught back, and leaves, like the after-image
   Released from the floor of a now different mind,
A quick gold, dyeing the uncovering beach
   With sunglaze. That which we were,
Confronted by all that we are not,
   Grasps in subservience its replenishment.

# WINTER ENCOUNTERS

House and hollow; village and valley-side:
    The ceaseless pairings, the interchange
In which the properties are constant
    Resumes its winter starkness. The hedges' barbs
Are bared. Lengthened shadows
    Intersecting, the fields seem parcelled smaller
As if by hedgerow within hedgerow. Meshed
    Into neighbourhood by such shifting ties,
The house reposes, squarely upon its acre
    Yet with softened angles, the responsive stone
Changeful beneath the changing light:
    There is a riding-forth, a voyage impending
In this ruffled air, where all moves
    Towards encounter. Inanimate or human,
The distinction fails in these brisk exchanges—
    Say, merely, that the roof greets the cloud,
Or by the wall, sheltering its knot of talkers,
    Encounter enacts itself in the conversation
On customary subjects, where the mind
    May lean at ease, weighing the prospect
Of another's presence. Rain
    And the probability of rain, tares
And their progress through a field of wheat—
    These, though of moment in themselves,
Serve rather to articulate the sense
    That having met, one meets with more
Than the words can witness. One feels behind
    Into the intensity that bodies through them
Calmness within the wind, the warmth in cold.

# OXEN: PLOUGHING AT FIESOLE

The heads, impenetrable
And the slow bulk
Soundless and stooping,
A white darkness—burdened
Only by sun, and not
By the matchwood yoke—
They groove in ease
The meadow through which they pace
Tractable. It is as if
Fresh from the escape,
They consent to submission,
The debris of captivity
Still clinging there
Unnoticed behind those backs:
'But we submit'—the tenor
Unambiguous in that stride
Of even confidence—
'Giving and not conceding
Your premises. Work
Is necessary, therefore—'
(With an unsevered motion
Holding the pauses
Between stride and stride)
'We will be useful
But we will not be swift: now
Follow us for your improvement
And at our pace.' This calm
Bred from this strength, and the reality
Broaching no such discussion,
The man will follow, each
As the other's servant
Content to remain content.

# THE MEDITERRANEAN

## I

In this country of grapes
Where the architecture
Plays musical interludes, flays
The emotions with the barest statement
Or, confusing the issue and the beholder,
Bewilders with an excessive formality,
There is also the sea.

## II

The sea
Whether it is 'wrinkled' and 'crawls'
Or pounds, plunders, rounding
On itself in thunderous showers, a
Broken, bellowing foam canopy
Rock-riven and driven wild
By its own formless griefs—the sea
Carries, midway, its burning stripe of light.

## III

This country of grapes
Is a country, also, of trains, planes and gasworks.
'Tramway and palace' rankles. It is an idea
Neither the guidebook nor the imagination
Tolerates. The guidebook half lies
Of 'twenty minutes in a comfortable bus'
Of 'rows of cypresses, an
Uninterrupted series of matchless sights'.
The imagination cannot lie. It bites brick;
Says: 'This is steel—I will taste steel.

Bred on a lie, I am merely
Guidebooks, advertisements, politics.'

The sea laps by the railroad tracks.
To have admitted this also defines the sea.


## HOW STILL THE HAWK


How still the hawk
Hangs innocent above
Its native wood:
Distance, that purifies the act
Of all intent, has graced
Intent with beauty.
Beauty must lie
As innocence must harm
Whose end (sited,
Held) is naked
Like the map it cowers on.
And the doom drops:
Plummet of peace
To him who does not share
The nearness and the need,
The shrivelled circle
Of magnetic fear.

# GLASS GRAIN

The glare goes down. The metal of a molten pane
Cast on the wall with red light burning through,
Holds in its firm, disordered square, the shifting strands
The glass conceals, till (splitting sun) it dances
Lanterns in lanes of light its own streaked image.
Like combed-down hair. Like weathered wood, where
Line, running with, crowds on line and swaying
Rounding each knot, yet still keeps keen
The perfect parallel. Like . . . in likes, what do we look for?
Distinctions? That, but not that in sum. Think of the fugue's
    theme:
After inversions and divisions, doors
That no keys can open, cornered conceits
Apprehensions, all ways of knowledge past,
Eden comes round again, the motive dips
Back to its shapely self, its naked nature
Clothed by comparison alone—related. We ask
No less, watching suggestions that a beam selects
From wood, from water, from a muslin-weave,
Swerving across our window, on our wall
(Transparency teased out) the grain of glass.

# TRAMONTANA AT LERICI

Today, should you let fall a glass it would
    Disintegrate, played off with such keenness
Against the cold's resonance (the sounds
    Hard, separate and distinct, dropping away
In a diminishing cadence) that you might swear
    This was the imitation of glass falling.

Leaf-dapples sharpen. Emboldened by this clarity
    The minds of artificers would turn prismatic,
Running on lace perforated in crisp wafers
    That could cut like steel. Constitutions,
Drafted under this fecund chill, would be annulled
    For the strictness of their equity, the moderation of their pity.

At evening, one is alarmed by such definition
    In as many lost greens as one will give glances to recover,
As many again which the landscape
    Absorbing into the steady dusk, condenses
From aquamarine to that slow indigo-pitch
    Where the light and twilight abandon themselves.

And the chill grows. In this air
    Unfit for politicians and romantics
Dark hardens from blue, effacing the windows:
    A tangible block, it will be no accessory
To that which does not concern it. One is ignored
    By so much cold suspended in so much night.


## NORTHERN SPRING


Nor is this the setting for extravagance. Trees
    Fight with the wind, the wind eludes them
Streaking its cross-lanes over the uneasy water
    Whose bronze whitens. To emulate such confusion
One must impoverish the resources of folly,
    But to taste it is medicinal. Consider

How through that broken calm, as the sun emerges,
    The sky flushes its blue, dyeing the grass
In the promise of a more stable tone:
    Less swift however than the cloud is wide—
Its shadow (already) quenching the verdure
    As its bulk muffles the sun—the blue drains
And the assault renews in colourless ripples.

Then, lit, the scene deepens. Where should one look
    In the profusion of possibilities? One conceives
Placing before them a square house
    Washed in the coolness of lime, a hub
For the scattered deployment, to define
    In pure white from its verdant ground
The variegated excess which threatens it.

Spring lours. Neither will the summer achieve
    That Roman season of an equable province
Where the sun is its own witness and the shadow
    Measures its ardour with the impartiality
Of the just. Evening, debauching this sky, asks
    To be appraised and to be withstood.


## THE CRANE


That insect, without antennae, over its
Cotton-spool lip, letting
An almost invisible tenuity
Of steel cable, drop
Some seventy feet, with the
Grappling hook hidden also
Behind a dense foreground
Among which it is fumbling, and
Over which, mantis-like

It is begging or threatening, gracile
From a clear sky—that paternal
Constructive insect, without antennae,
Would seem to assure us that
'The future is safe, because
It is in my hands.' And we do not
Doubt this veracity, we can only
Fear it—as many of us
As pause here to remark
Such silent solicitude
For lifting intangible weights
Into real walls.

## PARING THE APPLE

There are portraits and still-lifes.

And there is paring the apple.

And then? Paring it slowly,
From under cool-yellow
Cold-white emerging. And . . . ?

The spring of concentric peel
Unwinding off white,
The blade hidden, dividing.

There are portraits and still-lifes
And the first, because 'human'
Does not excel the second, and
Neither is less weighted
With a human gesture, than paring the apple
With a human stillness.

The cool blade
Severs between coolness, apple-rind
Compelling a recognition.

# MORE FOREIGN CITIES

*'Nobody wants any more poems about foreign cities . . .'*
*(From a recent disquisition on poetics)*

Not forgetting Ko-jen, that
Musical city (it has
Few buildings and annexes
Space by combating silence),
There is Fiordiligi, its sun-changes
Against walls of transparent stone
Unsettling all preconception—a city
For architects (they are taught
By casting their nets
Into those moving shoals); and there is
Kairouan, whose lit space
So slides into and fits
The stone masses, one would doubt
Which was the more solid
Unless, folding back
Gold segments out of the white
Pith globe of a quartered orange,
One may learn perhaps
To read such perspectives. At Luna
There is a city of bridges, where
Even the inhabitants are mindful
Of a shared privilege: a bridge
Does not exist for its own sake.
It commands vacancy.

# A MEDITATION ON JOHN CONSTABLE

*'Painting is a science, and should be pursued as an inquiry into the laws
of nature. Why, then, may not landscape painting be considered as a
branch of natural philosophy, of which pictures are but the experiments?'*
    John Constable, *The History of Landscape Painting*


He replied to his own question, and with the unmannered
    Exactness of art; enriched his premises
By confirming his practice: the labour of observation
    In face of meteorological fact. Clouds
Followed by others, temper the sun in passing
    Over and off it. Massed darks
Blotting it back, scattered and mellowed shafts
    Break damply out of them, until the source
Unmasks, floods its retreating bank
    With raw fire. One perceives (though scarcely)
The remnant clouds trailing across it
    In rags, and thinned to a gauze.
But the next will dam it. They loom past
    And narrow its blaze. It shrinks to a crescent
Crushed out, a still lengthening ooze
    As the mass thickens, though cannot exclude
Its silvered-yellow. The eclipse is sudden,
    Seen first on the darkening grass, then complete
In a covered sky.
                        Facts. And what are they?
He admired accidents, because governed by laws,
    Representing them (since the illusion was not his end)
As governed by feeling. The end is our approval
    Freely accorded, the illusion persuading us
That it exists as a human image. Caught
    By a wavering sun, or under a wind
Which moistening among the outlines of banked foliage
    Prepares to dissolve them, it must grow constant;

Though there, ruffling and parted, the disturbed
   Trees let through the distance, like white fog
Into their broken ranks. It must persuade
   And with a constancy, not to be swept back
To reveal what it half-conceals. Art is itself
   Once we accept it. The day veers. He would have judged
Exactly in such a light, that strides down
   Over the quick stains of cloud-shadows
Expunged now, by its conflagration of colour.
   A descriptive painter? If delight
Describes, which wrings from the brush
   The errors of a mind, so tempered,
It can forgo all pathos; for what he saw
   Discovered what he was, and the hand—unswayed
By the dictation of a single sense—
   Bodied the accurate and total knowledge
In a calligraphy of present pleasure. Art
   Is complete when it is human. It is human
Once the looped pigments, the pin-heads of light
   Securing space under their deft restrictions
Convince, as the index of a possible passion,
   As the adequate gauge, both of the passion
And its object. The artist lies
   For the improvement of truth. Believe him.


## FRONDES AGRESTES

*On re-reading Ruskin*


A leaf, catching the sun, transmits it:
'First a torch, then an emerald.'

'Compact, like one of its own cones':
The round tree with the pyramid shadow.

First the felicities, then
The feelings to appraise them:

Light, being in its untempered state,
A rarity, we are (says the sage) meant
To enjoy 'most probably' the effects of mist.

Nature's difficulties, her thought
Over dints and bosses, her attempts
To beautify with a leopard-skin of moss
The rocks she has already sculpted,
All disclose her purposes—the thrush's bill,
The shark's teeth, are not his story.

Sublimity is. One awaits its passing,
Organ voice dissolving among cloud wrack.
The climber returns. He brings
Sword-shaped, its narrowing strip
Fluted and green, the single grass-blade, or
Gathered up into its own translucence
Where there is no shade save colour, the unsymbolic rose.


## FAREWELL TO VAN GOGH


The quiet deepens. You will not persuade
    One leaf of the accomplished, steady, darkening
Chestnut-tower to displace itself
    With more of violence than the air supplies
When, gathering dusk, the pond brims evenly
    And we must be content with stillness.

Unhastening, daylight withdraws from us its shapes
    Into their central calm. Stone by stone
Your rhetoric is dispersed until the earth
    Becomes once more the earth, the leaves
A sharp partition against cooling blue.

Farewell, and for your instructive frenzy
    Gratitude. The world does not end tonight
And the fruit that we shall pick tomorrow
    Await us, weighing the unstripped bough.


## CÉZANNE AT AIX


And the mountain: each day
Immobile like fruit. Unlike, also
—Because irreducible, because
Neither a component of the delicious
And therefore questionable,
Nor distracted (as the sitter)
By his own pose and, therefore,
Doubly to be questioned: it is not
Posed. It is. Untaught
Unalterable, a stone bridgehead
To that which is tangible
Because unfelt before. There
In its weathered weight
Its silence silences, a presence
Which does not present itself.

# AT HOLWELL FARM

It is a quality of air, a temperate sharpness
    Causes an autumn fire to burn compact,
To cast from a shapely and unrifted core
    Its steady brightness. A kindred flame
Gathers within the stone, and such a season
    Fosters, then frees it in a single glow:
Pears by the wall and stone as ripe as pears
    Under the shell-hood's cornice; the door's
Bright oak, the windows' slim-cut frames
    Are of an equal whiteness. Crude stone
By a canopy of shell, each complements
    In opposition, each is bound
Into a pattern of utilities—this farm
    Also a house, this house a dwelling.
Rooted in more than earth, to dwell
    Is to discern the Eden image, to grasp
In a given place and guard it well
    Shielded in stone. Whether piety
Be natural, is neither the poet's
    Nor the builder's story, but a quality of air,
Such as surrounds and shapes an autumn fire
    Bringing these sharp disparities to bear.

# ON THE HALL AT STOWEY

Walking by map, I chose unwonted ground,
    A crooked, questionable path which led
Beyond the margin, then delivered me
    At a turn. Red marl
Had rutted the aimless track
    That firmly withheld the recompense it hid
Till now, close by its end, the day's discoveries
    Began with the dimming night:

A house. The wall-stones, brown.
    The doubtful light, more of a mist than light
Floating at hedge-height through the sodden fields
    Had yielded, or a final glare
Burst there, rather, to concentrate
    Sharp saffron, as the ebbing year—
Or so it seemed, for the dye deepened—poured
    All of its yellow strength through the way I went:

Over grass, garden-space, over the grange
    That jutted beyond, lengthening-down
The house line, tall as it was,
    By tying it to the earth, trying its pride
(Which submitted) under a nest of barns,
    A walled weight of lesser encumbrances—
Few of which worsened it, and none
    As the iron sheds, sealing my own approach.

All stone. I had passed these last, unwarrantable
    Symbols of—no; let me define, rather
The thing they were not, all that we cannot be,
    By the description, simply of that which merits it:

Stone. Why must (as it does at each turn)
    Each day, the mean rob us of patience, distract us
Before even its opposite?—before stone, which
    Cut, piled, mortared, is patience's presence.

The land farmed, the house was neglected: but
    Gashed panes (and there were many) still showed
Into the pride of that presence. I had reached
    Unchallenged, within feet of the door
Ill-painted, but at no distant date—the least
    Our prodigal time could grudge it; paused
To measure the love, to assess its object,
    That trusts for continuance to the mason's hand.

Five centuries—here were (at the least) five—
    In linked love, eager excrescence
Where the door, arched, crowned with acanthus,
    Aimed at a civil elegance, but hit
This sturdier compromise, neither Greek, Gothic
    Nor Strawberry, clumped from the arching-point
And swathing down, like a fist of wheat,
    The unconscious emblem for the house's worth.

Conclusion surrounded it, and the accumulation
    After Lammas growth. Still coming on
Hart's-tongue by maiden-hair
    Thickened beneath the hedges, the corn levelled
And carried, long-since; but the earth
    (Its tint glowed in the house wall)
Out of the reddish dark still thrust up foison
    Through the browning-back of the exhausted year:

Thrust through the unweeded yard, where earth and house
    Debated the terrain. My eye
Caught in those flags a gravestone's fragment
    Set by a careful century. The washed inscription

24

Still keen, showed only a fragile stem
    A stave, a broken circlet, as
(Unintelligibly clear, craft in the sharp decrepitude)
    A pothook grooved its firm memorial.

Within, wet from the failing roof,
    Walls greened. Each hearth refitted
For a suburban whim, each room
    Denied what it was, diminished thus
To a barbarous mean, had comforted (but for a time)
    Its latest tenant. Angered, I turned to my path
Through the inhuman light, light that a fish might swim
    Stained by the greyness of the smoking fields.

Five centuries. And we? What we had not
    Made ugly, we had laid waste—
Left (I should say) the office to nature
    Whose blind battery, best fitted to perform it
Outdoes us, completes by persistence
    All that our negligence fails in. Saddened,
Yet angered beyond sadness, where the road
    Doubled upon itself I halted, for a moment
Facing the empty house and its laden barns.


## CIVILITIES OF LAMPLIGHT


Without excess (no galaxies
Gauds, illiterate exclamations)
It betokens haven,
An ordering, the darkness held
But not dismissed. One man
Alone with his single light
Wading obscurity refines the instance,
Hollows the hedge-bound track, a sealed
Furrow on dark, closing behind him.

from 'Antecedents'

## VI SOMETHING: A DIRECTION

Out of the shut cell of that solitude there is
   One egress, past point of interrogation.
Sun is, because it is not you; you are
   Since you are self, and self delimited
Regarding sun. It downs? I claim? Cannot
   Beyond such speech as this, gather conviction?
Judge, as you will, not what I say
   But what is, being said. It downs
Recovered, coverless, in a shriven light
   And you, returning, may to a shriven self
As from the scene, your self withdraws. You are downing
   Back from that autumn music of the light, which
Split by your need, to know the textures of your pain,
   Refuses them in your acceptance. You accept
An evening, washed of its overtones
   By strict seclusion, yet are not secluded
Withheld at your proper bounds. From there
   Your returns may enter, welcome strangers
Into a civil country (you were not the first
   To see it), but a country, natural and profuse
Unbroken by past incursions, as the theme
   Strung over stave, is rediscovered
After dismemberment in the canon, and over stave
   Can still proceed, unwound, unwinding
To its established presence, its territory
   Staked and sung; and the phrase descends
As a phase concluded. Released
   From knowing to acknowledgement, from prison
To powers, you are new-found
   Neighboured, having earned relation

With all that is other. Still you must wait,
    For evening's ashen, like the slow fire
Withdrawn through the whitened log
    Glinting through grain marks where the wood splits:
Let be its being: the scene extends
    Not hope, but the urgency that hopes for means.


# THE CHURCHYARD WALL


Stone against stone, they are building back
    Round the steepled bulk, a wall
That enclosed from the neighbouring road
    The silent community of graves. James Bridle,
Jonathan Silk and Adam Bliss, you are well housed
    Dead, howsoever you lived—such headstones
Lettered and scrolled, and such a wall
    To repel the wind. The channel, first,
Dug to contain a base in solid earth
    And filled with the weightier fragments. The propped yews
Will scarcely outlast it; for, breached,
    It may be rebuilt. The graves weather
And the stone skulls, more ruinous
    Than art had made them, fade by their broken scrolls.
It protects the dead. The living regard it
    Once it is falling, and for the rest
Accept it. Again, the ivy
    Will clasp it down, save for the buried base
And that, where the frost has cracked,
    Must be trimmed, reset, and across its course
The barrier raised. Now they no longer
    Prepare: they build, judged by the dead.
The shales must fit, the skins of the wall-face
    Flush, but the rising stones

27

Sloped to the centre, balanced upon an incline.
    They work at ease, the shade drawn in
To the uncoped wall which casts it, unmindful
    For the moment, that they will be outlasted
By what they create, that their labour
    Must be undone. East and west
They cope it edgewise; to the south
    Where the talkers sit, taking its sun
When the sun has left it, they have lain
    The flat slabs that had fallen inwards
Mined by the ivy. They leave completed
    Their intent and useful labours to be ignored,
To pass into common life, a particle
    Of the unacknowledged sustenance of the eye,
Less serviceable than a house, but in a world of houses
    A merciful structure. The wall awaits decay.

# A Peopled Landscape (1963)

## WINTER-PIECE

You wake, all windows blind—embattled sprays
grained on the medieval glass.
Gates snap like gunshot
as you handle them. Five-barred fragility
sets flying fifteen rooks who go together
silently ravenous above this winter-piece
that will not feed them. They alight
beyond, scavenging, missing everything
but the bladed atmosphere, the white resistance.
Ruts with iron flanges track
through a hard decay
where you discern once more
oak-leaf by hawthorn, for the frost
rewhets their edges. In a perfect web
blanched along each spoke
and circle of its woven wheel,
the spider hangs, grasp unbroken
and death-masked in cold. Returning
you see the house glint-out behind
its holed and ragged glaze,
frost-fronds all streaming.

## CANAL

Swans. I watch them
come unsteadying
the dusty, green

and curving arm
of water. Sinuously
both the live
bird and the bird
the water bends
into a white and wandering
reflection of itself,
go by in grace
a world of objects.
Symmetrically punched
now empty rivet-
holes betray
a sleeper fence:
below its raggedness
the waters darken
and above it rear
the saw-toothed houses
which the swinging
of the waters makes
scarcely less regular
in repetition. Swans
are backed by these, as
these are by
a sky of silhouettes,
all black and almost
all, indefinite.
A whitish smoke
in drifting diagonals
accents, divides
the predominance of street
and chimney lines,
where all is either
mathematically supine
or vertical, except
the pyramids of slag.
And, there, unseen
among such angularities—
a church, a black

freestanding witness
that a space of graves
invisibly is also
there. Only
its clock identifies
the tower between
the accompaniment of stacks
where everything
repeats itself—
the slag, the streets
and water that repeats
them all again
and spreads them rippling
out beneath
the eye of the discriminating
swans that seek
for something else
and the blank brink
concludes them without conclusion.


## JOHN MAYDEW or THE ALLOTMENT


Ranges
    of clinker heaps
        go orange now:
through cooler air
    an acrid drift
        seeps upwards
from the valley mills;
    the spoiled and staled
        distances invade
these closer comities
    of vegetable shade,
        glass-houses, rows

and trellises of red-
    ly flowering beans.
        This
is a paradise
    where you may smell
        the cinders
of quotidian hell beneath you;
    here grow
        their green reprieves
for those
    who labour, linger in
        their watch-chained waistcoats
rolled-back sleeves—
    the ineradicable
        peasant in the dispossessed
and half-tamed Englishman.
    By day, he makes
        a burrow of necessity
from which
    at evening, he emerges
        here.
A thoughtful yet unthinking man,
    John Maydew,
        memory stagnates
in you and breeds
    a bitterness; it grew
        and rooted in your silence
from the day
    you came
        unwitting out of war
in all the pride
    of ribbons and a scar
        to forty years
of mean amends . . .
    He squats
        within his shadow

and a toad
    that takes
        into a slack and twitching jaw
the worms he proffers it,
    looks up at him
        through eyes that are
as dimly faithless
    as the going years.
        For, once returned
he found that he
    must choose between
        an England, profitlessly green
and this—
    a seamed and lunar grey
        where slag in lavafolds
unrolls beneath him.
    The valley gazes up
        through kindling eyes
as, unregarded at his back
    its hollows deepen
        with the black, extending shadows
and the sounds of day
    explore its coming cavities,
        the night's
refreshed recesses.
    Tomorrow
        he must feed its will,
his interrupted pastoral
    take heart into
        those close
and gritty certainties that lie
    a glowing ruse
        all washed in hesitations now.
He eyes the toad
    beating
        in the assuagement
of his truce.

# THE HAND AT CALLOW HILL FARM

Silence. The man defined
The quality, ate at his separate table
Silent, not because silence was enjoined
But was his nature. It shut him round
Even at outdoor tasks, his speech
Following upon a pause, as though
A hesitance to comply had checked it—
Yet comply he did, and willingly:
Pause and silence: both
Were essential graces, a reticence
Of the blood, whose calm concealed
The tutelary of that upland field.

# THE PICTURE OF J. T. IN A PROSPECT
## OF STONE

What should one
    wish a child
        and that, one's own
emerging
    from between
        the stone lips
of a sheep-stile
    that divides
        village graves
and village green?
    —Wish her
        the constancy of stone.
—But stone
    is hard.
        —Say, rather

it resists
     the slow corrosives
          and the flight
of time
     and yet it takes
          the play, the fluency
from light.
          —How would you know
               the gift you'd give
was the gift
     she'd wish to have?
          —Gift is giving,
gift is meaning:
     first
          I'd give
then let her
     live with it
          to prove
its quality the better and
     thus learn
          to love
what (to begin with)
     she might spurn.
          —You'd
moralize a gift?
     —I'd have her
          understand
the gift I gave her.
          —And so she shall
               but let her play
her innocence away
     emerging
          as she does
between
     her doom (unknown),
          her unmown green.

# UP AT LA SERRA

The shadow
    ran before it lengthening
        and a wave went over.
Distance
    did not obscure
        the machine of nature:
you could watch it
    squander and recompose itself
        all day, the shadow-run
the sway of the necessity down there
    at the cliff-base
        crushing white from blue.
Come in
    by the arch
        under the campanile parrocchiale
and the exasperation of the water
    followed you,
        its *Soldi, soldi*
unpicking the hill-top peace
    insistently.
        He knew, at twenty
all the deprivations such a place
    stored for the man
        who had no more to offer
than a sheaf of verse
    in the style of Quasimodo.
        Came the moment,
he would tell it
    in a poem
        without rancour, a lucid
testament above his name
    *Paolo*
        *Bertolani*

*—Ciao, Paolo!*
     *—Ciao*
          *Giorgino!*
He would put them
     all in it—
          Giorgino going
over the hill
     to look for labour;
          the grinder
of knives and scissors
     waiting to come up, until
          someone would hoist his wheel
on to a back, already
     hooped to take it,
          so you thought
the weight must crack
     the curvature. And then:
          Beppino and Beppino
friends
     who had in common
          nothing except their names and friendship;
and the sister of the one
     who played the accordion
          and under all
the *Soldi, soldi,*
     *sacra conversazione*
          *del mare—*
*della madre.*
     Sometimes
          the men had an air of stupefaction:
*La Madre:*
     it was the women there
          won in a truceless enmity.
At home
     a sepia-green
          *Madonna di Foligno*

shared the wall
     with the October calendar—
          Lenin looked out of it,
Mao
     blessing the tractors
          and you told
the visitors:
     *We are not communists*
          *although we call ourselves communists*
*we are what you English*
     *would call . . . socialists.*
          He believed
that God was a hypothesis,
     that the party would bring in
          a synthesis, that he
would edit the local paper for them,
     or perhaps
          go northward to Milan;
or would he grow
     as the others had—son
          to the puttana-madonna
in the curse,
     chafed by the maternal knot and by
          the dream of faithlessness,
uncalloused hands,
     lace, white
          at the windows of the sailors' brothels
in the port five miles away?
     *Soldi—*
          *soldi—*
some
     worked at the naval yards
          and some, like him
were left between
     the time the olives turned
          from green to black

and the harvest of the grapes,
     idle
          except for hacking wood.
Those
     with an acre of good land
          had vines, had wine
and self-respect. Some
     carried down crickets
          to the garden of the mad Englishwoman
who could
     not
          tolerate
crickets, and they received
     *soldi, soldi*
          for recapturing them . . .
The construction
     continued as heretofore
          on the villa of the Milanese dentist
as the evening
     came in with news:
          —*We have won*
*the election.*
     —*At the café*
          *the red flag is up.*
He turned back
     quickly beneath the tower.
          Giorgino
who wanted to be a waiter
     wanted to be commissar
          piling *sassi*
into the dentist's wall.
     Even the harlot's mother
          who had not dared
come forth because her daughter
     had erred in giving birth,
          appeared by the *Trattoria della Pace.*

She did not enter
	the masculine precinct,
		listening there, her shadow
lengthened-out behind her
	black as the uniform of age
		she wore
on back and head.
	This was the Day
		which began all reckonings
she heard them say
	with a woman's ears;
		she liked
the music from the wireless.
	The padre
		pulled
at his unheeded angelus
	and the Day went down behind
		the town in the bay below
where—come the season—
	they would be preparing
		with striped umbrellas,
for the *stranieri* and *milanesi*—
	treason so readily compounded
		by the promiscuous stir
on the iridescent sliding water.
	He had sought
		the clear air of the cliff.
—*Salve, Giorgino*
	—*Salve*
		*Paolo, have you*
*heard*
	*that we have won the election?*
		—*I am writing*
*a poem about it:*
	*it will begin*
		*here, with the cliff and with the sea*
*following its morning shadow in.*

# SEA POEM

A whiter bone:
    the sea-voice
        in a multiple monody
crowding towards that end.
    It is as if
        the transparencies of sound
composing such whiteness
    disposed many layers
        with a sole movement
of the various surface,
    the depths, bottle-glass green
        the bed, swaying
like a fault in the atmosphere, each
    shift
        with its separate whisper, each whisper
a breath of that singleness
    that 'moves together
        if it moves at all',
and its movement is ceaseless,
    and to one end—
        the grinding
a white bone.


# HEAD HEWN WITH AN AXE

The whittled crystal: fissured
For the invasion of shadows.

The stone book, its
Hacked leaves
Frozen in granite.

The meteorite, anatomized
By the geometer. And to what end?
To the enrichment of the alignment:
Sun against shade against sun:
That daily food, which
Were it not for such importunities
Would go untasted:

The suave block, desecrated
In six strokes. The light
Is staunching its wounds.


## OVER BROOKLYN BRIDGE


Mayakovsky
has it!—
       'in the place
of style, an austere
    disposition of bolts.'
      The poet cedes
his elocutionary function[1]
    to the telephone book:
      Helmann
Salinas
    Yarmolinsky,
      words
reciprocally
    kindling one another
      like the train of fire
over a jewel box.


[1] 'The poet cedes his elocutionary function . . .' is a slightly travestied
version of a famous passage from Mallarmé's *Crise de vers*: 'l'œuvre
pure implique la disparition élocutoire du poète, qui cède l'initiative
aux mots . . .'

Miss Moore
        had a negress
for a maid whose father
        was a Cherokee.
            'No', she said
'I do not live in town
        I live in Brooklyn.
            I was afraid
you wouldn't like it here—
        it's gotten so ugly.'
            I liked Brooklyn
with its survival
        of wooden houses
            and behind trees
the balconies colonnaded.
        And what I liked
            about the bridge
was the uncertainty
        the way
            the naked steel
would not go naked
        but must wear
            its piers of stone—
as the book says
        'stylistically
            its weakest feature'.
I like
        such weaknesses, the pull
            the stone base
gives to the armature.
        I live
            in a place of stone
if it's still there
        by the time I've sailed to it.
            Goodbye

Miss Moore
        I hope
                the peacock's feather you once saw
at the house of Ruskin
        has kept its variegations.
                Jewels
have histories:
        'I never did
                care for Mallarmé'
she said
        and the words
                in the book of names
are flames not bolts.


## ODE TO ARNOLD SCHOENBERG

*on a performance of his concerto for violin*


At its margin
        the river's double willow
                that the wind
variously
        disrupts, effaces
                and then restores
in shivering planes:
        it is
                calm morning.
The twelve notes
        (from the single root
                the double tree)
and their reflection:
        let there be
                unity—this,

however the winds rout
    or the wave disperses
        remains, as
in the liberation of the dissonance
    beauty would seem discredited
        and yet is not:
redefined
    it may be reachieved,
        thus to proceed
through discontinuities
    to the whole in which
        discontinuities are held
like the foam in chalcedony
    the stone, enriched
        by the tones' impurity.
The swayed mirror
    half-dissolves
        and the reflection
yields to reflected light.
    Day. The bell-clang
        goes down the air
and, like a glance
    grasping upon its single thread
        a disparate scene,
crosses and re-creates
    the audible morning.
        All meet at cockcrow
when our common sounds
    confirm our common bonds.
        Meshed in meaning
by what is natural
    we are discontented
        for what is more,
until the thread
    of an instrument pursue
        a more than common meaning.

But to redeem
       both the idiom and the instrument
             was reserved
to this exiled Jew—to bring
       by fiat
             certainty from possibility.
For what is sound
       made reintelligible
             but the unfolded word
branched and budded,
       the wintered tree
             creating, cradling space
and then
       filling it with verdure?

*American Scenes and Other Poems* (1966)

## THE SNOW FENCES

They are fencing the upland against
the drifts this wind, those clouds
would bury it under: brow and bone
know already that levelling zero
as you go, an aching skeleton,
in the breathtaking rareness of winter air.

Walking here, what do you see?
Little more, through wind-teased eyes,
than a black, iron tree
and, there, another, a straggle
of low and broken wall between, grass
sapped of its greenness, day going.

The farms are few: spread
as wide, perhaps, as when
the Saxons who found them, chose
these airy and woodless spaces
and froze here before they fed
the unsuperseded burial ground.

Ahead, the church's dead-white
limewash will dazzle the mind
as, dazed, you enter to escape:
despite the stillness here, the chill
of wash-light scarcely seems
less penetrant than the hill-top wind.

Between the graves, you find
a beheaded pigeon, the blood and grain
trailed from its bitten crop, as alien to all
the day's pallor as the raw
wounds of the earth, turned above
a fresh solitary burial.

A plaque of staining metal
distinguishes this grave among
an anonymity whose stones
the frosts have scaled, thrusting under
as if they grudged the ground
its ill-kept memorials.

The bitter darkness drives you
back valleywards, and again you bend
joint and tendon to encounter
the wind's force and leave behind
the nameless stones, the snow-shrouds
of a waste season: they are fencing
the upland against those years, those clouds.


## THE DOOR


Too little
has been said
of the door, its one
face turned to the night's
downpour and its other
to the shift and glisten of firelight.

Air, clasped
by this cover
into the room's book,

is filled by the turning
pages of dark and fire
as the wind shoulders the panels, or unsteadies that burning.

Not only
the storm's
breakwater, but the sudden
frontier to our concurrences, appearances,
and as full of the offer of space
as the view through a cromlech is.

For doors
are both frame and monument
to our spent time,
and too little
has been said
of our coming through and leaving by them.


## THE WEATHERCOCKS


Bitten and burned into mirrors of thin gold,
the weathercocks, blind from the weather,
have their days of seeing as they
grind round on their swivels.

A consciousness of pure metal
begins to melt when (say)
that light 'which never was'
begins to be

And catches the snow's accents
in each dip and lap, and the wide
stains on the thawed ploughland are like continents
across a rumpled map.

Their gold eyes hurt
at the corduroy lines come clear whose grain
feels its way over the shapes of the rises
joining one brown accord of stain and stain.

And the patterning stretches, flown
out on a wing of afternoon cloud that the sun
is changing to sea-wet sandflats,
hummocked in tiny dunes like the snow half-gone—

As if the sole wish of the light
were to harrow with mind matter, to shock
wide the glance of the tree-knots and the stone-eyes
the sun is bathing, to waken the weathercocks.


## A GIVEN GRACE

Two cups,
a given grace,
afloat and white
on the mahogany pool
of table. They unclench
the mind, filling it
with themselves.
Though common ware,
these rare reflections,
coolness of brown
so strengthens and refines
the burning of their white,
you would not wish
them other than they are—
you, who are challenged
and replenished by
those empty vessels.

# THE CAVERN

Obliterate
mythology as you unwind
this mountain-interior
into the negative-dark mind,
as there
the gypsum's snow
the limestone stair
and boneyard landscape grow
into the identity of flesh.

Pulse of the water-drop,
veils and scales, fins
and flakes of the forming
leprous rock,
how should these
inhuman, turn
human with such chill affinities?

Hard to the hand,
these mosses not of moss,
but nostrils, pits
of eyes, faces
in flight and prints
of feet where no feet ever were,
elude the mind's
hollow that would contain
this canyon within a mountain.

Not far
enough from the familiar,
press
in under a deeper dark until
the curtained sex
the arch, the streaming buttress
have become
the self's unnameable and shaping home.

# ARIZONA DESERT

Eye
drinks the dry orange ground,
the cowskull
bound to it by shade:
sun-warped, the layers
of flaked and broken bone
unclench into petals,
into eyelids of limestone:

Blind glitter
that sees
spaces and steppes expand
of the purgatories possible
to us and
impossible.

Upended trees
in the Hopi's desert orchard
betoken
unceasing unspoken war,
return
the levelling light,
imageless arbiter.

A dead snake
pulsates again
as, hidden, the beetles' hunger
mines through the tunnel of its drying skin.

Here, to be
is to sound
patience deviously
and follow
like the irregular corn
the water underground.

Villages
from mud and stone
parch back
to the dust they humanize
and mean
marriage, a loving lease
on sand, sun, rock and
Hopi
means peace.


## A DEATH IN THE DESERT

*in memory of Homer Vance*


There are no crosses
on the Hopi graves. They lie
shallowly
under a scattering
of small boulders. The sky
over the desert
with its sand-grain stars
and the immense equality

between
desert and desert sky,
seem
a scope and ritual
enough to stem
death and to be its equal.

'Homer
is the name,' said
the old Hopi doll-maker.
I met him in summer. He was dead
when I came back that autumn.

He had sat
like an Olympian
in his cool room
on the rock-roof of the world,
beyond the snatch
of circumstance
and was to die
beating a burro out of his corn-patch.

'That',
said his neighbour
'was a week ago.' And the week
that lay
uncrossably between us
stretched into sand,
into the spread
of the endless
waterless sea-bed beneath
whose space outpacing sight
receded as speechless and as wide as death.

# LAS TRAMPAS USA

*for Robert and Priscilla Bunker*

I go through hollyhocks
in a dry garden, up
to the house,
knock, then ask
in English for the key
to Las Trampas church.
The old woman
says in Spanish: I
do not speak English
so I say: Where
is the church key
in Spanish.
—You see those
three men working: you
ask them. She
goes in, I
go on
preparing to ask
them in Spanish:
Hi, they say
in American. Hello
I say and ask
them in English
where is the key
to the church and they
say: He has it
gesturing to a fourth
man working
hoeing a corn-field
nearby, and to him
(in Spanish): Where is
the church key? And he:
I have it.—O.K.
they say in

Spanish-American:
You bring it (and
to me in English)
He'll bring it. You
wait for him
by the church door.
Thank you, I say and they
reply in American
You're welcome. I go
once more and
await in shadow
the key: he
who brings it is not
he of the hoe, but
one of the three
men working, who
with a Castilian grace
ushers me in
to this place
of coolness out
of the August sun.


## MR BRODSKY


I had heard
before, of an
American who would have preferred
to be an Indian;
but not
until Mr Brodsky, of one
whose professed and long
pondered-on passion
was to become a Scot,
who even sent for haggis and oatcakes
across continent.

Having read him
in Cambridge English
a verse or two
from MacDiarmid,
I was invited
to repeat the reading
before a Burns Night Gathering
where the Balmoral Pipers
of Albuquerque would
play in the haggis
out of its New York tin.
Of course, I said
No. No. I could *not* go
and then
half-regretted I had not been.
But to console
and cure the wish, came
Mr Brodsky, bringing
his pipes and played
until the immense, distended
bladder of leather seemed
it could barely contain its water —
tears (idle
tears) for the bridal of Annie Laurie
and Morton J. Brodsky.
A bagpipe in a dwelling is
a resonant instrument
and there he stood
lost in the gorse
the heather or whatever
six thousand
miles and more
from the infection's source,
in our neo-New Mexican parlour
where I had heard
before of an
American who would have preferred
to be merely an Indian.

# UTE MOUNTAIN

'When I am gone'
the old chief said
'if you need me, call me',
and down he lay, became stone.

They were giants then
(as you may see),
and we
are not the shadows of such men.

The long splayed Indian hair
spread ravelling out
behind the rocky head
in groins, ravines;

petered across the desert plain
through Colorado,
transmitting force
in a single undulant unbroken line

from toe to hair-tip: there
profiled, inclined away from one
are features, foreshortened, and the high
blade of the cheekbone.

Reading it so, the eye
can take the entire great
straddle of mountain-mass,
passing down elbows, knees and feet.

'If you need me, call me.'
His singularity dominates the plain
as we call to our aid his image:
thus men make a mountain.

# A GARLAND FOR THOMAS EAKINS

*for Seymour Adelman*

### I

He lived
from his second year
at seventeen twentynine
Mount Vernon Street
Philadelphia
Pennsylvania where
he painted his
father and his sisters
and he died
in Pennsylvania in
Philadelphia at
seventeen twentynine
Mount Vernon Street.

### II

Anatomy, perspective
and reflection: a boat
in three inclinations:
to the wind, to the waves
and to the picture-frame.
Those are the problems. What
does a body propose
that a boat does not?

### III

Posing the model
for 'The Concert Singer' he
stood her
relative to a grid
placed vertically
behind her. There was a spot
before her
on the wall that

59

she must look at.
To her dress
by the intersections
of the grid he tied
coloured ribbons, thus
projecting her
like an architect's elevation
on a plane
that was vertical, the canvas
at a right angle
to the eye and perpendicular
to the floor.
What does the man
who sees
trust to
if not the eye? He trusts
to knowledge
to right appearances.

### IV
—And what do you think of
that, Mr Eakins? (A Whistler)
—I think that that
is a very cowardly way to paint.

### V
A fat woman
by Rubens
is not a fat
woman but a fiction.

## VI

The Eakins portrait
(said Whitman)
sets me down
in correct style
without feathers.
And when they
said to him:
Has Mr Eakins no
social gifts? he said
to them: What are
'social gifts'?—
The parlour puts
quite its own
measure upon social gifts.

## VII

The figures of perception
as against
the figures of elocution.
What they wanted
was to be Medici
in Philadelphia
and they survive
as Philadelphians.

## VIII

The accord with that
which asked
only to be recorded:
'How beautiful', he said,
'an old lady's skin is:
all those wrinkles!'

## IX

*Only*
to be recorded!
and his stare
in the self-portrait
calculates the abyss
in the proposition. He dies
unsatisfied, born
to the stubborn
anguish of
those eyes.


## THE WELL

*in a Mexican convent*


Leaning on
the parapet stone
Listening down
the long, dark
sheath through which the standing
shaft of water
sends its echoings up
Catching, as it stirs
the steady seethings
that mount and mingle
with surrounding sounds
from the neighbouring
barrack-yard: soldiery
—heirs, no doubt
of the gunnery that gashed
these walls of tattered
frescoes, the bullet-
holes now socketed
deeper by sunlight
and the bright gaps

giving on to the square
and there revealing
strollers in khaki
with their girls Aware
of a well-like
cool throughout
the entire, clear
sunlit ruin,
of the brilliant cupids
above the cistern
that hold up
a baldachin of stone
which is not there
Hearing the tide
of insurrection
subside through time
under the still-
painted slogans
*Hemos servido*
*lealmente*
*a la revolución*


## THE OAXACA BUS


*Fiat Voluntas Tua:*
over the head of the driver
an altar. No end to it,
the beginning seems to be
Our Lady of Solitude
blessing the crowd
out of a double frame—
gilt and green. Dark
mother by light,
her neighbour, the Guadalupe Virgin
is tucked away under the right-

63

hand edge as if
to make sure
twice over and (left)
are the legs of a protruding
post-card crucifixion
mothered by both. A cosmos
proliferates outwards
from the mystery, starts
with the minute, twin
sombreros dangling there, each
with embroidered brims
and a blood-red cord
circling the crown of each.
The driving mirror
catches their reflection, carries on
the miraculous composition
with two names —serifs
and flourishes—: *Maria,*
*Eugenia*: both
inscribed on the glass and
flanked at either end
by rampant rockets
torpedoing moonwards. Again
on either side,
an artificial vine
twines down: it is tied
to rails in the aisle
and, along it, flower—
are they nasturtiums? They are
pink like the bathing dresses
of the cut-out belles
it passes in descending,
their petals are pleated
like the green
of the fringed curtain that borders the windshield:
they are lilies
of the field of Mexico,
plastic godsend,

last flourish
of that first *Fiat* from sister goddesses
and ( yes)
the end . . .


# IDYLL

*Washington Square, San Francisco*


A door:
>>PER L'UNIVERSO
>>>>is what it says
above it.
>>>>You must approach
>>>>>>more nearly
(the statue
>>>>of Benjamin Franklin watching you)
>>>>>>before you see
*La Gloria di Colui*
>>>>*che tutto muove*
>>>>>>PER L'UNIVERSO
—leaning
>>>>along the lintel—
>>>>>>*penetra e risplende*
across this church
>>>>for Italian Catholics:
>>>>>>Dante
unscrolling in rhapsody.
>>>>Cool
>>>>>>the January sun.
that with an intensity
>>>>the presence of the sea
>>>>>>makes more exact,
chisels the verse with shade
>>>>and lays
>>>>>>on the grass

                a deep and even
                        Californian green,
                                while a brilliance
        throughout the square
                        flatters the meanness of its architecture.
                        Beyond
        there is the flood
                        which skirts this pond
                                and tugs the ear
        towards it: cars
                        thick on the gradients of the city
                                shift sun and sound—
        a constant ground-bass
                        to these provincialisms of the piazza
                                tasting still
        of Lerici and Genova.
                Here
                                as there
        the old men sit
                        in a mingled odour
                                of cheroot and garlic
        spitting;
                        they share serenity
                                with the cross-legged
        Chinese adolescent
                        seated between them
                                reading, and whose look
        wears the tranquility of consciousness
                        forgotten in its object—
                                his book
        bears for a title
                *SUCCESS*
                                *in spelling.*
        How
                        does one spell out this
                                *che penetra e risplende*

from square
                into the hill-side alley-ways
                                around it, where
between tall houses
                children of the Mediterranean
                                and Chinese element
mingle
                their American voices? . . .
                                The dictionary
defines idyllium
                as meaning
                                'a piece, descriptive
chiefly of rustic life';
                we
                                are in town: here
let it signify
                this poised quiescence, pause
                                and possibility in which
the music of the generations
                binds into its skein
                                the flowing instant,
while the winter sun
                pursues the shadow
                                before a church
whose decoration
                is a quotation from *Paradiso*.

# The Way of a World (1969)

## SWIMMING CHENANGO LAKE

Winter will bar the swimmer soon.
   He reads the water's autumnal hesitations
A wealth of ways: it is jarred,
   It is astir already despite its steadiness,
Where the first leaves at the first
   Tremor of the morning air have dropped
Anticipating him, launching their imprints
   Outwards in eccentric, overlapping circles.
There is a geometry of water, for this
   Squares off the clouds' redundances
And sets them floating in a nether atmosphere
   All angles and elongations: every tree
Appears a cypress as it stretches there
   And every bush that shows the season,
A shaft of fire. It is a geometry and not
   A fantasia of distorting forms, but each
Liquid variation answerable to the theme
   It makes away from, plays before:
It is a consistency, the grain of the pulsating flow.
   But he has looked long enough, and now
Body must recall the eye to its dependence
   As he scissors the waterscape apart
And sways it to tatters. Its coldness
   Holding him to itself, he grants the grasp,
For to swim is also to take hold
   On water's meaning, to move in its embrace
And to be, between grasp and grasping, free.
   He reaches in-and-through to that space
The body is heir to, making a where
   In water, a possession to be relinquished

Willingly at each stroke. The image he has torn
    Flows-to behind him, healing itself,
Lifting and lengthening, splayed like the feathers
    Down an immense wing whose darkening spread
Shadows his solitariness: alone, he is unnamed
    By this baptism, where only Chenango bears a name
In a lost language he begins to construe—
    A speech of densities and derisions, of half-
Replies to the questions his body must frame
    Frogwise across the all but penetrable element.
Human, he fronts it and, human, he draws back
    From the interior cold, the mercilessness
That yet shows a kind of mercy sustaining him.
    The last sun of the year is drying his skin
Above a surface a mere mosaic of tiny shatterings,
    Where a wind is unscaping all images in the flowing obsidian,
The going-elsewhere of ripples incessantly shaping.


## PROMETHEUS[1]


Summer thunder darkens, and its climbing
    Cumulae, disowning our scale in the zenith,
Electrify this music: the evening is falling apart.
    Castles-in-air; on earth: green, livid fire.
The radio simmers with static to the strains
    Of this mock last-day of nature and of art.


[1] 'Prometheus' refers to the tone-poem by Scriabin and to his hope
of transforming the world by music and rite.

We have lived through apocalypse too long:
    Scriabin's dinosaurs! Trombones for the transformation
That arrived by train at the Finland Station,
    To bury its hatchet after thirty years in the brain
Of Trotsky. Alexander Nikolayevitch, the events
    Were less merciful than your mob of instruments.

Too many drowning voices cram this waveband.
    I set Lenin's face by yours—
Yours, the fanatic ego of eccentricity against
    The systematic son of a schools inspector
Tyutchev on desk—for the strong man reads
    Poets as the antisemite pleads: 'A Jew was my friend.'

Cymballed firesweeps. Prometheus came down
    In more than orchestral flame and Kérensky fled
Before it. The babel of continents gnaws now
    And tears at the silk of those harmonies that seemed
So dangerous once. You dreamed an end
    Where the rose of the world would go out like a close in music.

Population drags the partitions down
    And we are a single town of warring suburbs:
I cannot hear such music for its consequence:
    Each sense was to have been reborn
Out of a storm of perfumes and light
    To a white world, an in-the-beginning.

In the beginning, the strong man reigns:
    Trotsky, was it not then you brought yourself
To judgement and to execution, when you forgot
    Where terror rules, justice turns arbitrary?
Chromatic Prometheus, myth of fire,
    It is history topples you in the zenith.

Blok, too, wrote The Scythians
　　Who should have known: he who howls
With the whirlwind, with the whirlwind goes down.
　　In this, was Lenin guiltier than you
When, out of a merciless patience grew
　　The daily prose such poetry prepares for?

Scriabin, Blok, men of extremes,
　　History treads out the music of your dreams
Through blood, and cannot close like this
　　In the perfection of anabasis. It stops. The trees
Continue raining though the rain has ceased
　　In a cooled world of incessant codas:

Hard edges of the houses press
　　On the after-music senses, and refuse to burn,
Where an ice cream van circulates the estate
　　Playing Greensleeves, and at the city's
Stale new frontier even ugliness
　　Rules with the cruel mercy of solidities.


## EDEN


I have seen Eden. It is a light of place
　　As much as the place itself; not a face
Only, but the expression on that face: the gift
　　Of forms constellates cliff and stones:
The wind is hurrying the clouds past,
　　And the clouds as they flee, ravelling-out
Shadow a salute where the thorn's barb
　　Catches the tossed, unroving sack
That echoes their flight. And the same
　　Wind stirs in the thicket of the lines
In Eden's wood, the radial avenues
　　Of light there, copious enough

71

To draft a city from. Eden
    Is given one, and the clairvoyant gift
Withdrawn, 'Tell us,' we say
    'The way to Eden', but lost in the meagre
Streets of our dispossession, where
    Shall we turn, when shall we put down
This insurrection of sorry roofs? Despair
    Of Eden is given, too: we earn
Neither its loss nor having. There is no
    Bridge but the thread of patience, no way
But the will to wish back Eden, this leaning
    To stand against the persuasions of a wind
That rings with its meaninglessness where it sang its meaning.


# ADAM


Adam, on such a morning, named the beasts:
    It was before the sin. It is again.
An openwork world of lights and ledges
    Stretches to the eyes' lip its cup:
Flower-maned beasts, beasts of the cloud,
    Beasts of the unseen, green beasts
Crowd forward to be named. Beasts of the qualities
    Claim them: sinuous, pungent, swift:
We tell them over, surround them
    In a world of sounds, and they are heard
Not drowned in them; we lay a hand
    Along the snakeshead, take up
The nameless muzzle, to assign its vocable
    And meaning. Are we the lords or limits
Of this teeming horde? We bring
    To a kind of birth all we can name
And, named, it echoes in us our being.
    Adam, on such a morning, knew

The perpetuity of Eden, drew from the words
    Of that long naming, his sense of its continuance
And of its source—beyond the curse of the bitten apple—
    Murmuring in wordless words: 'When you deny
The virtue of this place, then you
    Will blame the wind or the wide air,
Whatever cannot be mastered with a name,
    Mouther and unmaker, madman, Adam.'


## ASSASSIN

*'The rattle in Trotsky's throat and his wild boar's moans'*
                        *Piedra de Sol* (Octavio Paz)


Blood I foresaw. I had put by
    The distractions of the retina, the eye
That like a child must be fed and comforted
    With patterns, recognitions. The room
Had shrunk to a paperweight of glass and he
    To the centre and prisoner of its transparency.

He rasped pages. I knew too well
    The details of that head. I wiped
Clean the glance and saw
    Only his vulnerableness. Under my quivering
There was an ease, save for that starched insistence
    While paper snapped and crackled as in October air.

Sound drove out sight. We inhabited together
    One placeless cell. I must put down
This rage of the ear for discrimination, its absurd
    Dwelling on ripples, liquidities, fact
Fastening on the nerve gigantic paper burs.
    The gate of history is straiter than eye's or ear's.

In imagination, I had driven the spike
   Down and through. The skull had sagged in its blood.
The grip, the glance—stained but firm—
   Held all at its proper distance and now hold
This autumnal hallucination of white leaves
   From burying purpose in a storm of sibilance.

I strike. I am the future and my blow
   Will have it now. If lightning froze
It would hover as here, the room
   Riding in the crest of the moment's wave,
In the deed's time, the deed's transfiguration
   And as if that wave would never again recede.

The blood wells. Prepared for this
   This I can bear. But papers
Snow to the ground with a whispered roar:
   The voice, cleaving their crescendo, is his
Voice, and his the animal cry
   That has me then by the roots of the hair.

Fleshed in that sound, objects betray me,
   Objects are my judge: the table and its shadow,
Desk and chair, the ground a pressure
   Telling me where it is that I stand
Before wall and window-light:
   Mesh of the curtain, wood, metal, flesh:

A dying body that refuses death,
   He lurches against me in his warmth and weight,
As if my arm's length blow
   Had transmitted and spent its strength
Through blood and bone; and I, spectred,
   The body that rose against me were my own.

Woven from the hair of that bent head,
    The thread that I had grasped unlabyrinthed all—
Tightrope of history and necessity—
    But the weight of a world unsteadies my feet
And I fall into the lime and contaminations
    Of contingency; into hands, looks, time.


## AGAINST EXTREMITY


Let there be treaties, bridges,
    Chords under the hands, to be spanned
Sustained: extremity hates a given good
    Or a good gained. That girl who took
Her life almost, then wrote a book
    To exorcise and to exhibit the sin,
Praises a friend there for the end she made
    And each of them becomes a heroine.
The time is in love with endings. The time's
    Spoiled children threaten what they will do,
And those they cannot shake by petulance
    They'll bribe out of their wits by show.
Against extremity, let there be
    Such treaties as only time itself
Can ratify, a bond and test
    Of sequential days, and like the full
Moon slowly given to the night,
    A possession that is not to be possessed.

# IN THE FULLNESS OF TIME

*a letter to Octavio Paz*

The time you tell us is the century and the day
   Of Shiva and Parvati: imminent innocence,
Moment without movement. Tell us, too, the way
   Time, in its fullness, fills us
As it flows: tell us the beauty of succession
   That Breton denied: the day goes
Down, but there is time before it goes
   To negotiate a truce in time. We met
Sweating in Rome and in a place
   Of confusions, cases and telephones: and then
It was evening over Umbria, the train
   Arriving, the light leaving the dry fields
And next the approaching roofs. As we slowed
   Curving towards the station, the windows ahead swung
Back into our line of vision and flung at us
   A flash of pausing lights: the future
That had invited, waited for us there
   Where the first carriages were. That hesitant arc
We must complete by our consent to time —
   Segment to circle, chance into event:
And how should we not consent? For time
   Putting its terrors by, it was as if
The unhurried sunset were itself a courtesy.

# THE WAY OF A WORLD

Having mislaid it, and then
   Found again in a changed mind
The image of a gull the autumn gust
   Had pulled upwards and past
The window I watched from, I recovered too
   The ash-key, borne-by whirling
On the same surge of air, like an animate thing:
   The scene was there again: the bird,
The seed, the windlines drawn in the sidelong
   Sweep of leaves and branches that only
The black and supple boughs restrained—
   All would have joined in the weightless anarchy
Of air, but for that counterpoise. All rose
   Clear in the memory now, though memory did
     not choose
Or value it first: it came
   With its worth and, like those tree-tips,
Fine as dishevelling hair, but steadied
   And masted as they are, that worth
Outlasted its lost time, when
   The cross-currents had carried it under.
In all these evanescences of daily air,
   It is the shapes of change, and not the bare
Glancing vibrations, that vein and branch
   Through the moving textures: we grasp
The way of a world in the seed, the gull
   Swayed toiling against the two
Gravities that root and uproot the trees.

# DESCARTES AND THE STOVE

Thrusting its armoury of hot delight,
    Its negroid belly at him, how the whole
Contraption threatened to melt him
    Into recognition. Outside, the snow
Starkened all that snow was not—
    The boughs' nerve-net, angles and gables
Denting the brilliant hoods of it. The foot-print
    He had left on entering, had turned
To a firm dull gloss, and the chill
    Lined it with a fur of frost. Now
The last blaze of day was changing
    All white to yellow, filling
With bluish shade the slots and spoors
    Where, once again, badger and fox would wind
Through the phosphorescence. All leaned
    Into that frigid burning, corded tight
By the lightlines as the slow sun drew
    Away and down. The shadow, now,
Defined no longer: it filled, then overflowed
    Each fault in snow, dragged everything
Into its own anonymity of blue
    Becoming black. The great mind
Sat with his back to the unreasoning wind
    And doubted, doubted at his ear
The patter of ash and, beyond, the snow-bound farms,
    Flora of flame and iron contingency
And the moist reciprocation of his palms.

# ON THE PRINCIPLE OF
# BLOWCLOCKS

*Three-way Poem*[1]

*The static forces*
not a ball of silver
*of a solid body*
but a ball of air
*and its material strength*
whose globed sheernesses
*derive from*
shine with a twofold glitter:
*not the quantity of mass:*
once with the dew and once
*an engineer would instance*
with the constituent bright threads
*rails or T beams, say*
of all its spokes
*four planes constructed to*
in a tense surface
*contain the same volume as*
in a solid cloud of stars
*four tons of mass*

---

[1] A reading should include a) the italicized lines,
b) the unitalicized, c) the whole as printed.

# A SENSE OF DISTANCE

The door is shut.
The red rider
no longer crosses the canyon floor
under a thousand feet of air.

The glance that fell
on him, is shafting
a deeper well:
the boughs of the oak are roaring
inside the acorn shell.

The hoofbeats—silent, then—
are sounding now
that ride
dividing a later distance.

For I am in England,
and the mind's embrace
catches-up this English
and that horizonless desert space
into its own, and the three there
concentrically fill a single sphere.

And it seems as if a wind
had flung wide a door
above an abyss, where all
the kingdoms of possibilities shone
like sandgrains crystalline in the mind's own sun.

# THE FOX GALLERY

A long house—
the fox gallery you called
its upper storey, because
you could look down to see
(and did) the way a fox would
cross the field beyond
and you could follow out, window
to window, the fox's way
the whole length of the meadow
parallel with the restraining line
of wall and pane, or as far
as that could follow the sense of all
those windings. Do you remember
the morning I woke you with the cry
Fox fox and the animal
came on—not from side
to side, but straight
at the house and we craned
to see more and more, the most
we could of it and then
watched it sheer off deterred
by habitation, and saw
how utterly the two worlds were
disparate, as that perfect
ideogram for agility
and liquefaction flowed
away from us rhythmical
and flickering and
that flare was final.

# TO BE ENGRAVED
## ON THE SKULL OF A CORMORANT

across the thin
façade, the galleried-
with-membrane head:
narrowing, to take
the eye-dividing
declivity where
the beginning beak
prepares for flight
in a still-
perfect salience:
here, your glass
needs must stay
steady and your gross
needle re-tip
itself with reticence
but be
as searching as the sea
that picked and pared
this head yet spared
its frail acuity.

# THE CHANCES OF RHYME

The chances of rhyme are like the chances of meeting—
    In the finding fortuitous, but once found, binding:
They say, they signify and they succeed, where to succeed
    Means not success, but a way forward
If unmapped, a literal, not a royal succession;
    Though royal (it may be) is the adjective or region
That we, nature's royalty, are led into.
    Yes. We are led, though we seem to lead

Through a fair forest, an Arden (a rhyme
    For Eden)—breeding ground for beasts
Not bestial, but loyal and legendary, which is more
    Than nature's are. Yet why should we speak
Of art, of life, as if the one were all form
    And the other all Sturm-und-Drang? And I think
Too, we should confine to Crewe or to Mow
    Cop, all those who confuse the fortuitousness
Of art with something to be met with only
    At extremity's brink, reducing thus
Rhyme to a kind of rope's end, a glimpsed grass
    To be snatched at as we plunge past it—
Nostalgic, after all, for a hope deferred.
    To take chances, as to make rhymes
Is human, but between chance and impenitence
    (A half-rhyme) come dance, vigilance
And circumstance (meaning all that is there
    Besides you, when you are there). And between
Rest-in-peace and precipice,
    Inertia and perversion, come the varieties
Increase, lease, re-lease (in both
    Senses); and immersion, conversion—of inert
Mass, that is, into energies to combat confusion.
    Let rhyme be my conclusion.

# *Written on Water* (1972)

## ON WATER

'Furrow' is inexact:
no ship could be
converted to a plough
travelling this vitreous ebony:

seal it in sea-caves and
you cannot still it:
image on image bends
where half-lights fill it

with illegible depths
and lucid passages,
bestiary of stones,
book without pages:

and yet it confers
as much as it denies:
we are orphaned and fathered
by such solid vacancies:

## THE LIGHTHOUSE

The lighthouse is like the church of some island sect
    Who have known the mainland beliefs and have defected
Only to retain them in native purity
    And in the daily jubilation of storm and sea,

But adding every day new images
    To their liturgy of changes—each one
Some myth over and done with now
    Because sea has rebegotten land and land
The sea, and all is waiting to declare
    That things have never been praised for what they were,
                                                    emerging
Along promontory on enfiladed promontory.


## STONE SPEECH


Crowding this beach
are milkstones, white
teardrops; flints
edged out of flinthood
into smoothness chafe
against grainy ovals,
pitted pieces, nosestones,
stoppers and saddles;
veins of orange
inlay black beads:
chalk-swaddled babyshapes,
tiny fists, facestones
and facestone's brother
skullstone, roundheads
pierced by a single eye,
purple finds, all
rubbing shoulders:
a mob of grindings,
groundlings, scatterings
from a million necklaces
mined under sea-hills, the pebbles
are as various as the people.

# THE COMPACT: AT VOLTERRA

The crack in the stone, the black filament
   Reaching into the rockface unmasks
More history than Etruria or Rome
   Bequeathed this place. The ramparted town
Has long outlived all that; for what
   Are Caesar or Scipio beside
The incursion of the slow abyss, the daily
   Tribute the dry fields provide

Trickling down? There is a compact
   To undo the spot, between the unhurried sun
Edging beyond this scene, and the moon,
   Risen already, that has stained
Through with its pallor the remaining light:
   Unreal, that clarity of lips and wrinkles
Where shadow investigates each fold,
   Scaling the cliff to the silhouetted stronghold.

Civic and close-packed, the streets
   Cannot ignore this tale of unshorable earth
At the town brink; furrow, gully,
   And sandslide guide down
Each seeping rivulet only to deepen
   The cavities of thirst, dry out
The cenozoic skeleton, appearing, powdering away,
   Uncovering the chapped clay beneath it.

There is a compact between the cooling earth
   And every labyrinthine fault that mines it—
The thousand mouths whose language
   Is siftings, whisperings, rumours of downfall
That might, in a momentary unison,
   Silence all, tearing the roots of sound out
With a single roar: but the cicadas
   Chafe on, grapevine entwines the pergola

Gripping beyond itself. A sole farm
   Eyes space emptily. Those
Who abandoned it still wire
   Their vines between lopped willows:
Their terraces, fondling the soil together,
   Till up to the drop that which they stand to lose:
Refusing to give ground before they must,
   They pit their patience against the dust's vacuity.

The crack in the stone, the black filament
   Rooting itself in dreams, all live
At a truce, refuted, terracing; as if
   Unreasoned care were its own and our
Sufficient reason, to repair the night's derisions,
   Repay the day's delight, here where the pebbles
Of half-ripe grapes abide their season,
   Their fostering leaves outlined by unminding sky.

## AT SANT'ANTIMO

Flanking the place,
a cypress
stretches itself, its surface
working as the wind
travels it in a continual
breathing, an underwater
floating of foliage
upwards, till
compact and wavering
it flexes a sinuous
tip that chases
its own shadow
to and fro
across the still
stone tower.

# ARIADNE AND THE MINOTAUR[1]

When Theseus went down
she stood alone surrounded
by the sense of what finality it was
she entered now: the hot rocks offered her
neither resistance nor escape, but ran
viscous with the image of betrayal:
the pitted and unimaginable face
the minotaur haunted her with
kept forming there
along the seams and discolorations
and in the diamond sweat
of mica: the sword and thread
had been hers to give, and she
had given them, to this easer of destinies:
if she had gone
alone out of the sun and down where he
had threaded the way for her,
if she had gone
winding the ammonite of space
to where at the cold heart
from the dark stone the bestial warmth
would rise to meet her
unarmed in acquiescence, unprepared
her spindle of packthread ... her fingers felt now
for the image in the sunlit rock, and her ears
at the shock of touch took up a cry
out of the labyrinth
into their own, a groaning
that filled the stone mouth
hollowly: between the lips of stone
appeared he whom she had sent

[1] Suggested initially by Picasso's series of drawings, this ignores as
they do the question of the actual kinship between Ariadne and the
Minotaur. Perhaps she, too, was unaware of it.

to go where her unspeakable
intent unspoken had been to go
herself, and heaved unlabyrinthed at her feet
their mutual completed crime—
a put-by destiny, a dying
look that sought her
out of eyes the light extinguished,
eyes she should have led
herself to light: and the rays
that turned to emptiness in them
filling the whole of space with loss,
a waste of irrefutable sunlight spread
from Crete to Naxos.


# HAWKS


Hawks hovering, calling to each other
 Across the air, seem swung
Too high on the risen wind
 For the earth-clung contact of our world:
And yet we share with them that sense
 The season is bringing in, of all
The lengthening light is promising to exact
 From the obduracy of March. The pair,
After their kind are lovers and their cries
 Such as lovers alone exchange, and we
Though we cannot tell what it is they say,
 Caught up into their calling, are in their sway,
And ride where we cannot climb the steep
 And altering air, breathing the sweetness
Of our own excess, till we are kinned
 By space we never thought to enter
On capable wings to such reaches of desire.

## OF BEGINNING LIGHT

The light of the mind is poorer
than beginning light: the shades
we find pigment for
poor beside the tacit
variety we can all see
yet cannot say: of beginning light
I will say this, that it dispenses
imperial equality to everything
it touches, so that purple
becomes common wear, but purple
resolving in its chord
a thousand tones
tinged by a thousand
shadows, all
yielding themselves
slowly up: and the mind,
feeling its way among
such hesitant distinctions,
is left behind as they
flare into certainties that
begin by ending them
in the light of day.

# AUTUMN PIECE

Baffled
by the choreography of the season
the eye could not
with certainty see
whether it was wind
stripping the leaves or
the leaves were struggling to be free:

They came at you
in decaying spirals
plucked flung and regathered by the same
force that was twisting
the scarves of the vapour trails
dragging all certainties out of course:

As the car resisted it
you felt it in either hand
commanding car, tree, sky,
master of chances,
and at a curve was a red
board said 'Danger':
I thought it said dancer.

# EVENT

Nothing is happening
Nothing

A waterdrop
Soundlessly shatters
A gossamer gives

Against this unused space
A bird
Might thoughtlessly try its voice
But no bird does

On the trodden ground
Footsteps
Are themselves more pulse than sound

At the return
A little drunk
On air

Aware that
Nothing
Is happening

# DURING RAIN

Between
slats of the garden
bench, and strung
to their undersides
ride clinging
raindrops, white
with transmitted
light as the bench
with paint: ranged
irregularly
seven staves of them
shine out
against the space
behind: untroubled
by the least breeze they
seem not to move
but one
by one as if
suddenly ripening
tug themselves free
and splash
down to be
replaced by an identical
and instant twin:
the longer you
look at it
the stillness proves
one flow unbroken
of new, false pearls,
dropped seeds of now
becoming then.

# The Way In and Other Poems (1974)

## THE WAY IN

The needle-point's swaying reminder
   Teeters at thirty, and the flexed foot
Keeps it there. Kerb-side signs
   For demolitions and new detours,
A propped pub, a corner lopped, all
   Bridle the pressures that guide the needle.

I thought I knew this place, this face
   A little worn, a little homely.
But the look that shadows softened
   And the light could grace, keeps flowing away from me
In daily change; its features, rendered down,
   Collapse expressionless, and the entire town

Sways in the fume of the pyre. Even the new
   And mannerless high risers tilt and wobble
Behind the deformations of acrid heat—
   A century's lath and rafters. Bulldozers
Gobble a street up, but already a future seethes
   As if it had waited in the crevices:

A race in transit, a nomad hierarchy:
   Cargoes of debris out of these ruins fill
Their buckled prams: their trucks and hand-carts wait
   To claim the dismantlings of a neighbourhood—
All that a grimy care from wastage gleans,
   From scrap-iron down to heaps of magazines.

Slowing, I see the faces of a pair
    Behind their load: he shoves and she
Trails after him, a sexagenarian Eve,
    Their punishment to number every hair
Of what remains. Their clothes come of their trade—
    They wear the cast-offs of a lost decade.

The place had failed them anyhow, and their pale
    Absorption staring past this time
And dusty space we occupy together,
    Gazes the new blocks down—not built for them;
But what they are looking at they do not see.
    No Eve, but mindless Mnemosyne,

She is our lady of the nameless metals, of things
    No hand has made, and no machine
Has cut to a nicety that takes the mark
    Of clean intention—at best, the guardian
Of all that our daily contact stales and fades,
    Rusty cages and lampless lampshades.

Perhaps those who have climbed into their towers
    Will eye it all differently, the city spread
In unforeseen configurations, and living with this,
    Will find that civility I can only miss—and yet
It will need more than talk and trees
    To coax a style from these disparities.

The needle-point's swaying reminder
    Teeters: I go with uncongealing traffic now
Out onto the cantilevered road, window on window
    Sucked backwards at the level of my wheels.
Is it patience or anger most renders the will keen?
    This is a daily discontent. This is the way in.

# AT STOKE

I have lived in a single landscape. Every tone
    And turn have had for their ground
These beginnings in grey-black: a land
    Too handled to be primary—all the same,
The first in feeling. I thought it once
    Too desolate, diminished and too tame
To be the foundation for anything. It straggles
    A haggard valley and lets through
Discouraged greennesses, lights from a pond or two.
    By ash-tips, or where the streets give out
In cindery in-betweens, the hills
    Swell up and free of it to where, behind
The whole vapoury, patched battlefield,
    The cows stand steaming in an acrid wind.
This place, the first to seize on my heart and eye,
    Has been their hornbook and their history.

# GLADSTONE STREET

It was the place to go in nineteen-thirty,
And so we went. A housemaid or two
Still lingered on at the bigger houses.
A miner and his family were the next
To follow us there, had scarcely settled in
When the wife began dying, whitely visible
Through the bay window in their double bed.
At the back, the garden vanished
Under grass and a ramshackle shed.
People were sure the street was going downhill.
It literally was: cracks in our hall
Opened as the house started to subside
Towards the mines beneath. Miners were everywhere

Under that cancerous hill. My mother swore
That you could hear them tapping away below
Of a quiet night. Miners unnerved her so
Ever since one sat beside her on the train
And soiled her with his pit dirt. But it wasn't miners
Undid the street. The housemaids lasted
Until the war, then fed the factories.
Flat-dwellers came and went, in the divided houses,
Mothers unwedded who couldn't pay their rent.
A race of gardeners died, and a generation
Hacked down the walls to park their cars
Where the flowers once were. It was there it showed,
The feeble-minded style of the neighbourhood
Gone gaudily mad in painted corrugations,
Botches of sad carpentry. The street front has scarcely changed.
No one has recorded the place.
Perhaps we shall become sociology. We have outpaced
Gladstone's century. We might have been novels.

## THE MARL PITS

It was a language of water, light and air
    I sought—to speak myself free of a world
Whose stoic lethargy seemed the one reply
    To horizons and to streets that blocked them back
In a monotone fume, a bloom of grey.
    I found my speech. The years return me
To tell of all that seasoned and imprisoned:
    I breathe familiar, sedimented air
From a landscape of disembowellings, underworlds
    Unearthed among the clay. Digging
The marl, they dug a second nature
    And water, seeping up to fill their pits,
Sheeted them to lakes that wink and shine
    Between tips and steeples, streets and waste

97

In slow reclaimings, shimmers, balancings,
    As if kindling Eden rescinded its own loss
And words and water came of the same source.

## AFTER A DEATH

A little ash, a painted rose, a name.
    A moonshell that the blinding sky
Puts out with winter blue, hangs
    Fragile at the edge of visibility. That space
Drawing the eye up to its sudden frontier
    Asks for a sense to read the whole
Reverted side of things. I wanted
    That height and prospect such as music brings—
Music or memory. Neither brought me here.
    This burial place straddles a green hill,
Chimneys and steeples plot the distances
    Spread vague below: only the sky
In its upper reaches keeps
    An untarnished January colour. Verse
Fronting that blaze, that blade,
    Turns to retrace the path of its dissatisfactions,
Thought coiled on thought, and only certain that
    Whatever can make bearable or bridge
The waste of air, a poem cannot.
    The husk of moon, risking the whole of space,
Seemingly sails it, frailly launched
    To its own death and fullness. We buried
A little ash. Time so broke you down,
    Your lost eyes, dry beneath
Their matted lashes, a painted rose
    Seems both to memorialize and mock
What you became. It picks your name out
    Written on the roll beside a verse—
Obstinate words: measured against the blue,
    They cannot conjure with the dead. Words,

Bringing that space to bear, that air
    Into each syllable we speak, bringing
An earnest to us of the portion
    We must inherit, what thought of that would give
The greater share of comfort, greater fear—
    To live forever, or to cease to live?
The imageless unnaming upper blue
    Defines a world, all images
Of endeavours uncompleted. Torn levels
    Of the land drop, street by street,
Pitted and pooled, its wounds
    Cleansed by a light, dealt out
With such impartiality you'd call it kindness,
    Blindly assuaging where assuagement goes unfelt.


# HILL WALK

*for Philippe and Anne-Marie Jaccottet*


Innumerable and unnameable, foreign flowers
    Of a reluctant April climbed the slopes
Beside us. Among them, rosemary and thyme
    Assuaged the coldness of the air, their fragrance
So intense, it seemed as if the thought
    Of that day's rarity had sharpened sense, as now
It sharpens memory. And yet such pungencies
    Are there an affair of every day—Provençal
Commonplaces, like the walls, recalling
    In their broken sinuousness, our own
Limestone barriers, half undone
    By time, and patched against its sure effacement
To retain the lineaments of a place.
    In our walk, time used us well that rhymed
With its own herbs. We crested idly
    That hill of ilexes and savours to emerge

Along the plateau at last whose granite
    Gave on to air: it showed us then
The place we had started from and the day
    Half gone, measured against the distances
That lay beneath, a territory travelled.
    All stretched to the first fold
Of that unending landscape where we trace
    Through circuits, drops and terraces
The outworks, ruinous and overgrown,
    Where space on space has labyrinthed past time:
The unseizable citadel glimmering back at us,
    We contemplated no assault, no easy victory:
Fragility seemed sufficiency that day
    Where we sat by the abyss, and saw each hill
Crowned with its habitations and its crumbled stronghold
    In the scents of inconstant April, in its cold.


## HOW FAR

How far from us
even the nearest are
among these close leaves
crowding the window:

what we know
of that slow then sudden
bursting into green is merely
what we have seen of it and not

(fermenting at its heart)
darkness such as the blind might hear:
for us, there is no way in where
across these surfaces

the light is a white lie
told only to hide the dark
extent from us
of a seafloor continent.


## OF LADY GRANGE


Of Lady Grange
        that ill-starred daughter
        of Chiesly of Dalry: he
        who when the Lord President
        sat in adverse judgement
        murdered him:

She inherited
        the violence of her father, was married
        some say against her will, others
        so that she might spy on him
        to Erskine, my Lord Grange,
        Jacobite, profligate and bigot:

He
        and the family she bore him
        detested her: but when a separation
        was arranged, my Lady Grange went on
        molesting him, opposed as she was
        to his politics and his person:

One night—
        it was a decade and more
        after the rebellion and its failure—
        her husband and his friends
        gathered, each to rehearse his part
        in the restoration of the house of Stuart:

The lives
        of men of great family
        were at stake when she, concealed
        it is said beneath a sofa
        or a day-bed where they sat,
        burst forth and threatened to betray them:

James Erskine
        judging her capable of that,
        two gentlemen (attended)
        called at her lodging: her resistance
        cost her two teeth as they forced her
        first into a sedan, then on to horse:

Her husband
        had it given out that she
        was sick of a fever: the next day
        she 'died' of it and he
        saw to it that her funeral should
        have all of the ceremony due to blood:

Her journey
        was as cold as the earth
        her coffin lay in:
        air, spray and the spread of water
        awaited the living woman
        her stone mocked greyly:

They rode
        from Edinburgh to Stirling and despite
        storms, robbers, Highland
        tracks and the lack of them,
        reached the deserted Castle Tirrim
        at Moidart loch:

Thence
>on by boat, and out
>into the Atlantic: Heiskir
>was to house her two years,
>until the single family there
>could no longer tolerate her

And said so:
>from a ship, two men
>appeared and carried her
>on board to Kilda, where
>no one could speak her language,
>nor would she learn theirs:

She learned
>to spin and in a clew
>of yarn sent with her neighbours' wool
>to Inverness, she hid a message,
>though she had neither pen nor pencil:
>this was the sixth year of her exile:

To Hope,
>her misnamed lawyer,
>the letter seemed
>to be written in blood: a ship
>chartered, fitted and sent
>found without its tenant

The house
>on Kilda, chimneyless, earth-floored:
>for her, once more
>the inevitable sea, Skye
>at last and the sand of a sea-cave
>where fish-nets hung to dry

At Idrigill:
>nor could this place
>keep the secret long:
>though the cliffs hung sheer,
>the fishers came
>to cure their catch and to sleep here:

Again
>she must be moved on
>and over to Uist: a large
>boulder, knotted in a noose,
>lay in the boat: a guard stood
>ready to sink his charge

If
>rounding a headland of the cliff
>the ship, sighting them,
>should pursue: out into the surge
>oars drew them where
>the three wrecked women

Emerge
>from the sea in stone:
>they were set for the further isles:
>Bracadale sank down
>behind them into its mist:
>now they could only trust

Time
>to weary what vigilance
>might try, and time
>so ruffled and so smoothed
>the sea-lanes they went by,
>was it from Uist, Harris or Assynt

That she
        came back to Skye?
        Of the life she had
        in Vaternish, all we hear
        is of the madness of her last
        and fifteenth year

In exile,
        of 'the poor, strange lady
        who came ashore
        and died', and of the great
        funeral which the Macleod
        of Ramsay's portrait, paid for:

Yet still
        no ordinary end
        attended that lonely woman:
        'for reasons unknown'
        the coffin at Duirinish
        held stones only:

But there
        where Kilconan church
        still points at variable skies
        a roofless gable, the square
        stone of a later year
        confesses her corpse:

She
        is well buried above that sea,
        the older dead beside her
        murdered in the burning church
        and, below, their slayers on the same
        day slain, the dyke-wall toppled to cover them.

# The Shaft (1978)

## CHARLOTTE CORDAY

*'O Vertu! le poignard, seul espoir de la terre,*
*Est ton arme sacrée . . .'*

—Chénier

Courteously self-assured, although alone,
With voice and features that could do no hurt,
Why should she not enter? They let in
A girl whose reading made a heroine—
Her book was Plutarch, her republic Rome:
Home was where she sought her tyrant out.

The towelled head next, the huge batrachian mouth:
There was a mildness in him, even. He
Had never been a woman's enemy,
And time and sickness turned his stomach now
From random execution. All the same,
He moved aside to write her victims down,
And when she approached, it was to kill she came.

She struck him from above. One thrust. Her whole
Intent and innocence directing it
To breach through flesh and enter where it must,
It seemed a blow that rose up from within:
Tinville[1] reduced it all to expertise:
—What, would you make of me a hired assassin?

[1] Fouquier Tinville was the public prosecutor.

106

—What did you find to hate in him?—His crimes.
Every reply was temperate save one
And that was human when all's said and done:
The deposition, read to those who sit
In judgement on her, 'What has she to say?'
'Nothing, except that I succeeded in it.'

—You think that you have killed all Marats off?
—I think perhaps such men are now afraid.
The blade hung in its grooves. How should she know
The Terror still to come, as she was led
Red-smocked from gaol out into evening's red?
It was to have brought peace, that faultless blow.

Uncowed by the unimaginable result,
She loomed by in the cart beneath the eye
Of Danton, Desmoulins and Robespierre,
Heads in a rabble fecund in insult:
She had remade her calendar, called this
The Fourth Day of the Preparation of Peace.

*Greater than Brutus* was what Adam Lux
Demanded for her statue's sole inscription:
His pamphlet was heroic and absurd
And asked the privilege of dying too:
Though the republic raised to her no statue,
The brisk tribunal took him at his word.

What haunted that composure none could fault?
For she, when shown the knife, had dropped her glance—
She 'who believed her death would raise up France'
As Chénier wrote who joined the later dead:
Her judge had asked: 'If you had gone uncaught,
Would you have then escaped?' 'I would,' she said.

A daggered Virtue, Clio's roll of stone,
Action unsinewed into statuary!
Beneath that gaze what tremor was willed down?
And, where the scaffold's shadow stretched its length,
What unlived life would struggle up against
Death died in the possession of such strength?

Perhaps it was the memory of that cry
That cost her most as Catherine Marat
Broke off her testimony ... But the blade
Inherited the future now and she
Entered a darkness where no irony
Seeps through to move the pity of her shade.


## FOR DANTON

'Bound to the fierce Metropolis ...'
—Wordsworth, *The Prelude*, Book X

*In the autumn of 1793 —the year in which he had instituted
the Revolutionary Tribunal —Danton went back to his birth-
place, Arcis-sur-Aube. After his return in November, he was
to be arrested, tried and condemned.*

Who is the man that stands against this bridge
And thinks that he and not the river advances?
Can he not hear the links of consequence
Chiming his life away? Water is time.
Not yet, not yet. He fronts the parapet
Drinking the present with unguarded sense:

The stream comes on. Its music deafens him
To other sounds, to past and future wrong.
The beat is regular beneath that song.
He hears in it a pulse that is his own;
He hears the year autumnal and complete.
November waits for him who has not done

With seeings, savourings. Grape-harvest brings
The south into the north. This parapet
Carries him forward still, a ship from Rheims,
From where, in boyhood and on foot, he'd gone
'To see,' he said, 'the way a king is made',
The king that he himself was to uncrown—

Destroyed and superseded, then secure
In the possession of a perfect power
Returned to this: to river, town and plain,
Walked in the fields and knew what power he'd lost,
The cost to him of that metropolis where
He must come back to rule and Robespierre.

Not yet. This contrary perfection he
Must taste into a life he has no time
To live, a lingered, snatched maturity
Before he catches in the waterchime
The measure and the chain a death began,
And fate that loves the symmetry of rhyme
Will spring the trap whose teeth must have a man.

# CASAROLA

*for Attilio Bertolucci*

Cliffs come sheering down into woodland here:
    The trees—they are chestnuts—spread to a further drop
Where an arm of water rushes through unseen
    Still lost in leaves: you can hear it
Squandering its way towards the mill
    A path crossing a hillslope and a bridge
Leads to at last: the stones lie there
    Idle beside it: they were cut from the cliff
And the same stone rises in wall and roof
    Not of the mill alone, but of shed on shed
Whose mossed tiles like a city of the dead
    Grow green in the wood. There are no dead here
And the living no longer come
    In October to crop the trees: the chestnuts
Dropping, feed the roots they rose from:
    A rough shrine sanctifies the purposes
These doors once opened to, a desolation
    Of still-perfect masonry. There is a beauty
In this abandonment: there would be more
    In the slow activity of smoke
Seeping at roof and lintel; out of each low
    Unwindowed room rising to fill
Full with essences the winter wood
    As the racked crop dried. Waste
Is our way. An old man
    Has been gathering mushrooms. He pauses
To show his spoil, plumped by a soil
    Whose sweet flour goes unmilled:
Rapid and unintelligible, he thinks we follow
    As we feel for his invitations to yes and no:
Perhaps it's the mushrooms he's telling over
    Or this place that shaped his dialect, and where nature
Daily takes the distinctness from that signature
    Men had left there in stone and wood,
Among waning villages, above the cities of the plain.

# PROSE POEM

*for John and Lisbeth*

If objects are of two kinds—those
    That we contemplate and, the remainder, use,
I am unsure whether its poetry or prose
    First drew us to this jar. A century
Ago, an apothecary must have been its owner,
    Thankful that it was airtight. And in spite of time
It remains so still. Its cylinder of glass,
    Perfectly seamless, has the finality and satisfaction
Of the achieved act of an artisan. Indeed,
    The stopper of ground glass, that refused
To be freed from the containing neck,
    Was almost too well-made. What had to be done
If we were to undo it, was to pass
    A silk cord round the collar of glass
And rub it warm—but this friction
    Must be swift enough not to conduct its heat
Inside—the best protection against which
    (Only a third hand can ensure this feat)
Is a cube of ice on top of the stopper.
    Whether it was the rubbing only, or the warm
Grasp that must secure the bottle's body,
    The stopper, once more refusing at first,
Suddenly parted—breathed-out
    (So to speak) by the warmed expanding glass.
Remaining ice-cool itself, when
    Lightly oiled, it was now ready again
For use—but not before we had tried
    Jar against ear to find the sound inside it.
It gave off—no seashell murmur—
    A low, crystalline roar that wholly
Possessed one's cavities, a note (as it were)
    Of unfathomable distance—not emptiness,
For this dialogue between air and ear
    Was so full of electric imponderables, it could compare

111

Only with that molecular stealth when the jar
   Had breathed. There is one sole lack
Now that jar and stopper are in right relation—
   An identifiable aroma: what we must do
Is to fill it with coffee, for use, scent and contemplation.


## IMAGES OF PERFECTION


               . . . What do we see
   In the perfect thing? Is our seeing
Merely a measuring, a satisfaction
   To be compared? How do we know at sight
And for what they are, these rarenesses
   That are right? In yesterday's sky
Every variety of cloud accompanied earth,
   Mares' tails riding past mountainous anvils,
While their shadows expunged our own:
   It was pure display—all a sky could put on
In a single day, and yet remain sky.
   I mean, you felt in the air the sway
Of sudden apocalypse, complete revelation:
   But what it came to was a lingering
At the edge of time, a perfect neighbouring,
   Until the twilight brought it consummation,
Seeping in violet through the entire scene.
   Where was the meaning, then? Did Eden
Greet us ungated? Or was that marrying
   Purely imaginary and, if it were,
What do we see in the perfect thing?

# THE FARING

That day, the house was so much a ship
   Clasped by the wind, the whole sky
Piling its cloud-wrack past,
   To be sure you were on dry land
You must go out and stand in that stream
   Of air: the entire world out there
Was travelling too: in each gap the tides
   Of space felt for the earth's ship sides:
Over fields, new-turned, the cry
   And scattered constellations of the gulls
Were messengers from that unending sea, the sky:
   White on brown, a double lambency
Pulsed, played where the birds, intent
   On nothing more than the ploughland's nourishment,
Brought the immeasurable in: wing on wing
   Taking new lustres from the turning year
Above seasonable fields, they tacked and climbed
   With a planet's travelling, rhymed here with elsewhere
In the sea-salt freshnesses of tint and air.


# THE METAMORPHOSIS

Bluebells come crowding a fellside
   A stream once veined. It rises
Like water again where, bell on bell,
   They flow through its bed, each rope
And rivulet, each tributary thread
   Found-out by flowers. And not the slope
Alone, runs with this imaginary water:
   Marshes and pools of it stay
On the valley-floor, fed (so the eye would say)
   From the same store and streamhead.

Like water, too, this blueness not all blue
   Goes ravelled with groundshades, grass and stem,
As the wind dishevels and strokes it open;
   So that the mind, in salutary confusion,
Surrendering up its powers to the illusion,
   Could, swimming in metamorphoses, believe
Water itself might move like a flowing of flowers.


## MUSHROOMS

*for Jon and Jill*

Eyeing the grass for mushrooms, you will find
A stone or stain, a dandelion puff
Deceive your eyes—their colour is enough
To plump the image out to mushroom size
And lead you through illusion to a rind
That's true—flint, fleck or feather. With no haste
Scent-out the earthy musk, the firm moist white,
And, played-with rather than deluded, waste
None of the sleights of seeing: taste the sight
You gaze unsure of—a resemblance, too,
Is real and all its likes and links stay true
To the weft of seeing. You, to begin with,
May be taken in, taken beyond, that is,
This place of chiaroscuro that seemed clear,
For realer than a myth of clarities
Are the meanings that you read and are not there:
Soon, in the twilight coolness, you will come
To the circle that you seek and, one by one,
Stooping into their fragrance, break and gather,
Your way a winding where the rest lead on
Like stepping stones across a grass of water.

# SKY WRITING

A plane goes by,
and the sky takes hold
on the frail, high chalk-line
of its vapour-trail, picks
it apart, combs out
and spreads the filaments
down either side
the spine of a giant plume
which rides written on air now:
that flocculent, unwieldy sceptre
begins its sway with
an essential uncertainty, a
veiled threat tottering it
slowly to ruin, and the sky
grasping its tatters
teases them thin,
letting in blue until,
all flaxen cobblings, lit
transparencies, they
give up their ghosts
to air, lost in their opposite.

# IN ARDEN

*'This is the forest of Arden . . .'*

Arden is not Eden, but Eden's rhyme:
   Time spent in Arden is time at risk
And place, also: for Arden lies under threat:
   Ownership will get what it can for Arden's trees:
No acreage of green-belt complacencies
   Can keep Macadam out: Eden lies guarded:
Pardonable Adam, denied its gate,
   Walks the grass in a less-than-Eden light
And whiteness that shines from a stone burns with his fate:
   Sun is tautening the field's edge shadowline
Along the wood beyond: but the contraries
   Of this place are contrarily unclear:
A haze beats back the summer sheen
   Into a chiaroscuro of the heat:
The down on the seeded grass that beards
   Each rise where it meets with sky,
Ripples a gentle fume: a fine
   Incense, smelling of hay smokes by:
Adam in Arden tastes its replenishings:
   Through its dense heats the depths of Arden's springs
Convey echoic waters—voices
   Of the place that rises through this place
Overflowing, as it brims its surfaces
   In runes and hidden rhymes, in chords and keys
Where Adam, Eden, Arden run together
   And time itself must beat to the cadence of this river.

# THE SHAFT

*for Guy Davenport*

The shaft seemed like a place of sacrifice:
   You climbed where spoil heaps from the hill
Spilled out into a wood, the slate
   Tinkling underfoot like shards, and then
You bent to enter: a passageway:
   Cervix of stone: the tick of waterdrops,
A clear clepsydra: and squeezing through
   Emerged into cathedral space, held-up
By a single rocksheaf, a gerbe
   Buttressing-back the roof. The shaft
Opened beneath it, all its levels
   Lost in a hundred feet of water.
Those miners—dust, beards, mattocks—
   They photographed seventy years ago,
Might well have gone to ground here, pharaohs
   Awaiting excavation, their drowned equipment
Laid-out beside them. All you could see
   Was rock reflections tunneling the floor
That water covered, a vertical unfathomed,
   A vertigo that dropped through centuries
To the first who broke into these fells:
   The shaft was not a place to stare into
Or not for long: the adit you entered by
   Filtered a leaf-light, a phosphorescence,
Doubled by water to a tremulous fire
   And signalling you back to the moist door
Into whose darkness you had turned aside
   Out of the sun of an unfinished summer.

# THE SCREAM

Night. A dream so drowned my mind,
　　Slowly it rose towards that sound,
Hearing no scream in it, but a high
　　Thin note, such as wasp or fly
Whines-out when spider comes dancing down
　　To inspect its net. Curtains—
I dragged them back—muffled the cry:
　　It rang in the room, but I could find
No web, wasp, fly. Blackly
　　Beyond the pane, the same sound
Met the ear and, whichever way
　　You pried for its source, seemed to be everywhere.
Torch, stair, door: the black
　　Was wavering in the first suffusion
Of the small hours' light. But nothing
　　Came clearly out of that obscure
Past-midnight, unshaped world, except
　　The shrill of this savaging. I struck uphill
And, caught in the torchbeam, saw
　　A lustre of eye, a dazzle on tooth
And stripe: badger above its prey
　　Glared worrying at that strident thing
It could neither kill nor silence. It swung
　　Round to confront the light and me,
Sinewed, it seemed, for the attack, until
　　I flung at it, stoned it back
And away from whatever it was that still
　　Screamed on, hidden in greyness. A dream
Had delivered me to this, and a dream
　　Once more seemed to possess one's mind,
For light could not find an embodiment for that scream,
　　Though it found the very spot and tussock
That relentlessly breathed and heaved it forth.
　　Was it a sound half-underground? Would badger

Bury its prey? Thoughts like these
　　No thoughts at all, crowded together
To appall the mind with dream uncertainties.
　　I flashed at the spot. It took reason
To unknot the ravel that hindered thought,
　　And reason could distinguish what was there,
But could no more bear the cry
　　Than the untaught ear. It was the tussock lived
And turned, now, at the touch of sight
　　—You could eye the lice among its spines—
To a hedgehog. Terrible in the denial
　　Of all comfort, it howled on here
For the lease that was granted it, the life
　　That was safe, and which it could not feel
Was its own yet. It howled down death
　　So that death might meet with its equal
Ten times the size of the despised life
　　It had hunted for. In this comedy
Under the high night, this refusal
　　To die with a taciturn, final dignity
A wolf's death, the scream
　　In its nest of fleas took on the sky.

# The Flood (1981)

## SNOW SIGNS

They say it is waiting for more, the snow
   Shrunk up to the shadow-line of walls
In an arctic smouldering, an unclean salt,
   And will not go until the frost returns
Sharpening the stars, and the fresh snow falls
   Piling its drifts in scallops, furls. I say
Snow has left its own white geometry
   To measure out for the eye the way
The land may lie where a too cursory reading
   Discovers only dip and incline leading
To incline, dip, and misses the fortuitous
   Full variety a hillside spreads for us:
It is written here in sign and exclamation,
   Touched-in contour and chalk-followed fold,
Lines and circles finding their completion
   In figures less certain, figures that yet take hold
On features that would stay hidden but for them:
   Walking, we waken these at every turn,
Waken ourselves, so that our walking seems
   To rouse some massive sleeper out of winter dreams
Whose stretching startles the whole land into life,
   As if it were us the cold, keen signs were seeking
To pleasure and remeasure, repossess
   With a sense in the gathered coldness of heat and height.
Well, if it's for more the snow is waiting
   To claim back into disguisal overnight,
As though it were promising a protection
   From all it has transfigured, scored and bared,
Now we shall know the force of what resurrection
   Outwaits the simplification of the snow.

# THEIR VOICES RANG

Their voices rang
through the winter trees:
they were speaking and yet it seemed they sang,
the trunks a hall of victory.

And what is that and where?
Though we come to it rarely,
the sense of all that we might be
conjures the place from air.

Is it the mind, then?
It is the mind received,
assumed into a season
forestial in the absence of all leaves.

Their voices rang
through the winter trees and time
catching the cadence of that song
forgot itself in them.


# FOR MIRIAM

### I

I climbed to your high village through the snow,
    Stepping and slipping over lost terrain:
Wind having stripped a dead field of its white
    Had piled the height beyond: I saw no way
But hung there wrapped in breath, my body beating:
    Edging the drift, trying it for depth.
Touch taught the body how to go
    Through straitest places. Nothing too steep

Or narrow now, once mind and muscle
    Learned to dance their balancings, combined
Against the misdirections of the snow.
    And soon the ground I gained delivered me
Before your smokeless house, and still
    I failed to read that sign. Through cutting air
Two hawks patrolled the reaches of the day,
    Black silhouettes against the sheen
That blinded me. How should I know
    The cold which tempered that blue steel
Claimed you already, for you were old.

## II

Mindful of your death, I hear the leap
    At life in the *resurrexit* of Bruckner's mass:
For, there, your hope towers whole:
    Within a body one cannot see, it climbs
That spaceless space, the ear's
    Chief mystery and mind's, that probes to know
What sense might feel, could it outgo
    Its own destruction, spiralling tireless
Like these sounds. To walk would be enough
    And top that rise behind your house
Where the land lies sheer to Wales,
    And Severn's crescent empties and refills
Flashing its sign inland, its pulse
    Of light that shimmers off the Atlantic:
For too long, age had kept you from that sight
    And now it beats within my eye, its pressure
A reply to the vein's own music
    Here, where with flight-lines interlinking
That sink only to twine and hover the higher,
    A circling of hawks recalls to us our chains
And snow remaining hardens above your grave.

## III

You wanted a witness that the body
    Time now taught you to distrust
Had once been good. 'My face,' you said—
    And the Shulamite stirred in decembering flesh
As embers fitfully relit—'My face
    Was never beautiful, but my hair
(It reached then to my knees) was beautiful.'
    We met for conversation, not conversion,
For you were that creature Johnson bridled at—
    A woman preacher. With age, your heresies
Had so multiplied that even I
    A pagan, pleaded for poetry forgone:
You thought the telling-over of God's names
    Three-fold banality, for what you sought
Was single, not (and the flame was in your cheek)
    'A nursery rhyme, a jingle for theologians.'
And the incarnation? That, too, required
    All of the rhetoric that I could bring
To its defence. The frozen ground
    Opened to receive you a slot in snow,
Re-froze, and months unborn now wait
    To take you into the earthdark disincarnate.

## IV

A false spring. By noon the frost
    Whitens the shadows only and the stones
Where they lie away from light. The fields
    Give back an odour out of earth
Smoking up through the haysmells where the hay
    —I thought it was sunlight in its scattered brightness—
Brings last year's sun to cattle wintering:
    The dark will powder them with white, and day
Discover the steaming herd, as beam
    On beam, and bird by bird, it thaws
Towards another noon. *Et resurrexit:*
    All will resurrect once more,

But whether you will rise again—unless
　To enter the earthflesh and its fullness
Is to rise in the unending metamorphosis
　Through soil and stem . . . This valediction is a requiem.
What was the promise to Abraham and his seed?
　That they should feed an everlasting life
In earthdark and in sunlight on the leaf
　Beyond the need of hope or help. But we
Would hunger in hope at the shimmer of a straw,
　Although it burned, a mere memory of fire,
Although the beauty of earth were all there were.


V

In summer's heat, under a great tree
　I hear the hawks cry down.
The beauty of earth, the memory of your fire
　Tell of a year gone by and more
Bringing the leaves to light: they spread
　Between these words and the birds that hang
Unseen in predatory flight. Again,
　Your high house is in living hands
And what we were saying there is what was said.
　My body measures the ground beneath me
Warm in this beech-foot shade, my verse
　Pacing out the path I shall not follow
To where you spoke once with a wounded
　And wondering contempt against your flock,
Your mind crowded with eagerness and anger.
　The hawks come circling unappeasably. Their clangour
Seems like the energy of loss. It is hunger.
　It pierces and pieces together, a single note,
The territories they come floating over now:
　The escarpment, the foreshore and the sea;
The year that has been, the year to be;
　Leaf on leaf, a century's increment
That has quickened and weathered, withered on the tree
　Down into this brown circle where the shadows thicken.

# HAY

The air at evening thickens with a scent
That walls exude and dreams turn lavish on—
Dark incense of a solar sacrament
Where, laid in swathes, the field-silk dulls and dries
To contour out the land's declivities
With parallels of grass, sweet avenues:
Scent hangs perpetual above the changes,
As when the hay is turned and we must lose
This clarity of sweeps and terraces
Until the bales space out the slopes again
Like scattered megaliths. Each year the men
Pile them up close before they build the stack,
Leaving against the sky, as night comes on,
A henge of hay-bales to confuse the track
Of time, and out of which the smoking dews
Draw odours solid as the huge deception.


## UNDER THE BRIDGE

Where the ranch-house disappeared its garden
seeded and the narcissi
began through a slow mutation
to breed smaller and smaller stars
unimpaired in scent: beside these
the horns of the cala lilies
each scroll protruding an insistent
yellow pistil seem from their scale
and succulent whiteness to belong
to an earlier world:
if there were men in it the trellises
that brace these stanchions
would fit the scale

of their husbandry and
if they made music it would
shudder and rebound
like that which travels down
the metal to the base
of this giant instrument
bedded among teazle, fennel, grass
in a returning wilderness
under the bridge

*San Francisco*

## SAN FRUTTUOSO:
### THE DIVERS

Seasalt has rusted the ironwork trellis
at the one café. Today
the bathers are all sun-bathers
and their bodies, side by side,
hide the minute beach:
the sea is rough and the sun's
rays pierce merely fitfully
an ill-lit sky. Unvisited,
the sellers of lace and postcards
have nothing to do, and the Dorias
in their cool tombs under the cloisters
sleep out history unfleshed.
*Oggi pesce spada*
says the café sign, but we
shall eat no swordfish today:
we leave by the ferry
from which the divers are arriving.
We wait under an orange tree
that produces flowers but no oranges.
They litter the rocks with their gear

126

and begin to assume
alternative bodies, slipping
into black rubbery skins with *Caution*
written across them.
They are of both sexes. They strap on
waist weights, frog feet,
cylinders of oxygen,
they lean their heaviness which water will lighten
back against rock, resting there
like burdened seals.
They test their cylinders
and the oxygen hisses at them.
They carry knives
and are well equipped to encounter
whatever it is draws them downwards
in their sleek black flesh.
The postcards show Christ—
*Cristo del mare*—
sunk and standing on his pedestal
with two divers circling
as airy as under-water birds
in baroque, ecstatic devotion
round the bad statue.
Will they find calm down there
we wonder, stepping heavily
over the ship-side gap,
feeling already the unbalancing
pull of the water under us.
We pass the granular rocks
faulted with long scars.
The sea is bristling up to them.
The straightness of the horizon
as we heave towards it
only disguises the intervening
sea-roll and sea-chop, the clutching glitter.
I rather like
the buck of the boat. What I dislike
with the sea tilting at us

is the thought of losing one's brains
as one slides sideways
to be flung at the bulwarks
as if weightless, the 'as if'
dissolving on impact
into bone and blood.
The maternal hand tightens
on the push-chair
that motion is dragging at:
her strapped-in child is asleep.
Perhaps those invisible divers—
luckier than we are—
all weight gone
levitate now
around the statue,
their corps de ballet
like Correggio's sky-
swimming angels, a swarm
of batrachian legs:
they are buoyed up by adoration,
the water merely an accidental aid
to such staggeringly
slow-motion pirouettes
forgetful of body, of gravity.
The sea-lurch snatches
and spins the wheels of his chair
and the child travels the sudden gradient
caught at by other hands,
reversed in mid-flight
and returned across the up-
hill deck to his mother:
a visitor,
she has the placid
and faintly bovine look
of a Northern madonna
and is scarcely surprised; he, too,
stays perfectly collected
aware now of what it was he had forgotten

while sleeping—the stuff
he was chewing from a packet,
which he continues to do.
He has come back to his body once more.
How well he inhabits his flesh:
lordly in unconcern,
he is as well accoutred as those divers.
He rides out the storm chewing and watching,
trustfully unaware
we could well go down
—though we do not, for already
the town is hanging above
us and the calm quay water.
From the roofs up there
perhaps one could see the divers
emerging, immersing,
whatever it is they are at
as we glide forward
up to the solid, deck to dock,
with salted lips.
The same sea
which wrecked Shelley
goes on rocking behind
and within us, hiding
its Christ, its swordfish,
as the coast reveals
a man-made welcome to us
of wall, street, room,
body's own measure and harbour,
shadow of lintel, portal
asking it in.

# ABOVE CARRARA

*for Paolo and Francesco*

Climbing to Colonnata past ravines
    Squared by the quarryman, geometric gulfs
Stepping the steep, the wire and gear
    Men use to pare a mountain: climbing
With the eye the absences where green should be,
    The annihilating scree, the dirty snow
Of marble, at last we gained a level
    In the barren flat of a piazza, leaned
And drank from the fountain there a jet
    As cold as tunneled rock. The place—
Plane above plane and block on block—
    Invited us to climb once more
And, cooled now, so we did
    Deep between church- and house-wall,
Up by a shadowed stairway to emerge
    Where the village ended. As we looked back then
The whole place seemed a quarry for living in,
    And between the acts of quarrying and building
To set a frontier, a nominal petty thing,
    While, far below, water that cooled our thirst
Dyed to a meal now, a sawdust flow,
    Poured down to slake those blades
Slicing inching the luminous mass away
    Above Carrara . . .

# FIREFLIES

The signal light of the firefly in the rose:
Silent explosions, low suffusions, fire
Of the flesh-tones where the phosphorous touches
On petal and on fold: that close world lies
Pulsing within its halo, glows or goes:
But the air above teems with the circulation
Of tiny stars on darkness, cosmos grows
Out of their circlings that never quite declare
The shapes they seem to pin-point, swarming there
Like stitches of light that fleck and thread a sea,
Yet unlike, too, in that the dark is spaces,
Its surfaces all surfaces seen through,
Discovered depths, filled by a flowering,
And though the rose lie lost now to the eye,
You could suppose the whole of darkness a forming rose.


# THUNDER IN TUSCANY

Down the façade lean statues listening:
Ship of the lightning-gust, ship of the night,
The long nave draws them into dark, they glisten
White in the rainflash, to shudder-out blackbright:
The threads of lightning net and re-sinew form
In sudden fragments—line of a mouth, a hem—
Taut with the intent a body shapes through them
Standing on sheerness outlistening the storm.

# THE LITTLETON WHALE

*in memory of Charles Olson*

What you wrote to know
was whether
the old ship canal
still paralleled the river
south
of Gloucester (England) . . .

What I never told
in my reply
was of the morning
on that same stretch
(it was a cold
January day in '85)
when Isobel Durnell
saw the whale . . .

She was up at dawn
to get her man off on time
to the brickyard and
humping up over the banks
beyond Bunny Row
a slate-grey hill showed
that the night before
had not been there . . .

They both ran outside
and down to the shore:
the wind was blowing
as it always blows
so hard that the tide
comes creeping up under it
often unheard . . .

The great grey-blue thing
had an eye
that watched wearily
their miniature motions as they
debated its fate
for the tide
was already feeling beneath it
floating it away . . .

It was Moses White
master mariner
owner of the sloop *Matilda*
who said the thing to do
was to get chains and a traction engine
—they got two from Olveston—
and drag it ashore:
the thing was a gift:
before long it would be
drifting off to another part of the coast
and lost to them
if they didn't move now . . .

And so the whale—
flukes, flesh, tail
trembling no longer
with a failing life—
was chained and hauled
installed above the tideline . . .

And the crowds came
to where it lay
upside down
displaying a
belly evenly-wrinkled
its eye lost to view
mouth skewed and opening into
an interior of tongue and giant sieves
that had once

filtered that diet of shrimp
its deep-sea sonar
had hunted out for it
by listening to submarine echoes
too slight
for electronic selection . . .

And Hector Knapp
wrote in his diary:
Thear was a Whal
cum ashore at Littleton Pill
and bid thear a fortnight
He was sixty eaight feet long
His mouth was twelve feet
The Queen claim it at last
and sould it for forty pound
Thear supposed to be
forty thousen pepeal to se it
from all parts of the cuntry . . .

The Methodist preacher
said that George Sindry
who was a very religious man
told himself when that whale came in
he'd heard so many arguments
about the tale of Jonah not being true
that he went to Littleton to
'satisfy people'. He was a tall man
a six footer
'but I got into that whale's mouth' he said
'and I stood in it
upright . . .'

The carcass
had overstayed its welcome
so they sent up a sizeable boat
to tow it to Bristol

and put it on show there
before they cut the thing down stinking
to be sold
and spread for manure . . .

You can still see the sign
to Whale Wharf as they renamed it
and Wintle's Brickworks became
the Whale Brick
Tile and Pottery Works . . .

Walking daily onto
the now-gone premises
through the 'pasture land
with valuable deposits of clay thereunder'
when the machine- and drying sheds
the five kilns, the stores and stables
stood permanent in that place
of their disappearance
Enoch Durnell still
relished his part in all that history begun
when Bella shook
and woke him with a tale that the tide
had washed up a whole house
with blue slates on it into Littleton Pill
and that house was a whale . . .


## THE FLOOD


It was the night of the flood first took away
    My trust in stone. Perfectly reconciled it lay
Together with water—and does so still—
    In the hill-top conduits that feed into
Cisterns of stone, cisterns echoing
    With a married murmur, as either finds

Its own true note in such a unison.
    It rained for thirty days. Down chimneys
And through doors, the house filled up
    With the roar of waters. The trees were bare,
With nothing to keep in the threat
    And music of that climbing, chiming din
Now rivers ran where the streams once were.
    Daily, we heard the distance lessening
Between house and water-course. But floods
    Occur only along the further plains and we
Had weathered the like of this before
    —The like, but not the equal, as we saw,
Watching it lap the enclosure wall,
    Then topping it, begin to pile across
And drop with a splash like clapping hands
    And spread. It took in the garden
Bed by bed, finding a level to its liking.
    The house-wall, fronting it, was blind
And therefore safe: it was the doors
    On the other side unnerved my mind
—They and the deepening night. I dragged
    Sacks, full of a mush of soil
Dug in the rain, and bagged each threshold.
    Spade in hand, why should I not make
Channels to guide the water back
    Into the river, before my barricade
Proved how weak it was? So I began
    Feeling my way into the moonless rain,
Hacking a direction. It was then as though
    A series of sluices had been freed to overflow
All the land beneath them: it was the dark I dug
    Not soil. The sludge melted away from one
And would not take the form of a trench.
    This work led nowhere, with no bed

To the flood, no end to its sources and resources
   To grow and to go wherever it would
Taking one with it. It was the sound
   Struck more terror than the groundlessness I trod,
The filth fleeing my spade—though that, too,
   Carried its image inward of the dissolution
Such sound orchestrates—a day
   Without reprieve, a swealing away
Past shape and self. I went inside.
   Our ark of stone seemed warm within
And welcoming, yet echoed like a cave
   To the risen river whose tide already
Pressed close against the further side
   Of the unwindowed wall. There was work to do
Here better than digging mud—snatching
   And carrying such objects as the flood
Might seep into, putting a stair
   Between the world of books and water.
The mind, once it has learned to fear
   Each midnight eventuality,
Can scarcely seize on what is already there:
   It was the feet first knew
The element weariness had wandered through
   Eyeless and unreasoning. Awakened eyes
Told that the soil-sacked door
   Still held, but saw then, without looking,
Water had tried stone and found it wanting:
   Wall fountained a hundred jets:
Floor lay awash, an invitation
   To water to follow it deriding door
On door until it occupied the entire house.
   We bailed through an open window, brushing
And bucketing with a mindless fervour
   As though four hands could somehow find
Strength to keep pace, then oversway
   The easy redundance of a mill-race. I say
That night diminished my trust in stone—
   As porous as a sponge, where once I'd seen

The image of a constancy, a ground for the play
    And fluency of light. That night diminished
Yet did not quite betray my trust.
    For the walls held. As we tried to sleep,
And sometimes did, we knew that the flood
    Rivered ten feet beneath us. And so we hung
Between a dream of fear and the very thing.
    Water-lights coursed the brain and sound
Turned it to the tympanum of an ear. When I rose
    The rain had ceased. Full morning
Floated and raced with water through the house,
    Dancing in whorls on every ceiling
As I advanced. Sheer foolishness
    It seemed to pause and praise the shimmer
And yet I did and called you down
    To share this vertigo of sunbeams everywhere,
As if no surface were safe from swaying
    And the very stone were as malleable as clay.
Primeval light undated the day
    Back into origin, washed past stain
And staleness, to a beginning glimmer
    That stilled one's beating ear to sound
Until the flood-water seemed to stream
    With no more burden than the gleam itself.
Light stilled the mind, then showed it what to do
    Where the work of an hour or two could
Hack a bank-side down, let through
    The stream and thus stem half the force
That carried its weight and water out of course.
    Strength spent, we returned. By night
The house was safe once more, but cold within.
    The voice of waters burrowed one's dream
Of ending in a wreck of walls:
    We were still here, with too much to begin
That work might make half-good.
    We waited upon the weather's mercies
And the December stars frosted above the flood.

# THE EPILOGUE

It was a dream delivered the epilogue:
　　I saw the world end: I saw
Myself and you, tenacious and exposed,
　　Smallest insects on the largest leaf:
A high trail coasted a ravine
　　Eyes could not penetrate because a wood
Hung down its slope: a fugue of water
　　Startled the ear and air with distances
Around and under us, as if a flood
　　Came pouring in from every quarter:
Our trail and height failed suddenly,
　　Fell sheer away into a visibility
More terrible than what the trees might hide:
　　Fed by a fall, wide, rising
Was it a sea? claimed all the plain
　　And climbed towards us, smooth
And ungainsayable. We turned and knew now
　　That no law steadied a sliding world,
For what we saw was an advancing wave
　　Cresting along the height. An elate
Despair held us together silent there
　　Waiting for that wall to fall and bury
Us and the love that taught us to forget
　　To fear it. I woke then to this room
Where first I heard the sounds that dogged that dream,
　　Caught back from epilogue to epilogue.

## Notes from New York and Other Poems (1984)

### ABOVE MANHATTAN

Up in the air
among the Iroquois[1]: no:
they are not born
with a head for heights:
their girder-going
is a learned, at last
a learnèd thing
as sure as instinct:
beneath them
they can see in print
the news sheet of the city
with a single rent where three
columns, clipped out of it,
show the Park was planted:
webbed and cradled
by the catenary
distances of bridge on bridge
the place is as real
as something imaginary:
but from where they are
one must read with care:
for to put
one foot wrong
is to drop
more than a glance

---

[1] The Iroquois are employed in high construction work.

and though
this closeness and that distance
make dancing difficult a dance
it is that the mind is led
above Manhattan


## ALL AFTERNOON


All afternoon the shadows have been building
A city of their own within the streets,
Carefully correcting the perspectives
With dark diagonals, and paring back
Sidewalks into catwalks, strips of bright
Companionways, as if it were a ship
This counter-city. But the leaning, black
Enjambements like ladders for assault
Scale the façades and tie them to the earth,
Confounding fire-escapes already meshed
In slatted ambiguities. You touch
The sliding shapes to find which place is which
And grime a finger with the ash of time
That blows through both, the shadow in the shade
And in the light, that scours each thoroughfare
To pit the walls, rise out of yard and stairwell
And tarnish the Chrysler's Aztec pinnacle.


## TO IVOR GURNEY


Driving north, I catch the hillshapes, Gurney,
    Whose drops and rises—Cotswold and Malvern
In their cantilena above the plains—
    Sustained your melody: your melody sustains

Them, now—Edens that lay
   Either side of this interminable roadway.
You would recognise them still, but the lanes
   Of lights that fill the lowlands, brim
To the Severn and glow into the heights.
   You can regain the gate: the angel with the sword
Illuminates the paths to let you see
   That night is never to be restored
To Eden and England spangled in bright chains.


## BLACK BROOK


Black Brook is brown. It travels
   With the hillside in it—an upside-down
Horizon above a brackened slope—until
   It drops and then: rags and a rush of foam
Whiten the peat-stained stream
   That keeps changing note and singing
The song of its shingle, its shallowness or its falls.
   I pace a parallel track to that of the water:
It must be the light of a moorland winter
   Let them say that black was fair name
For such a stream, making it mirror
   Solely the granite and the grey
As no doubt it can. But look! Black Brook
   Has its horizon back, and a blue
Inverted sky dyeing it through to a bed
   Of dazzling sand, an ore of gravel
It has washed out beneath rock and rowan
   As it came here homing down
To the valley it brightens belying its name.

# POEM FOR MY FATHER

I bring to countryside my father's sense
Of an exile ended when he fished his way
Along the stained canal and out between
The first farms, the uninterrupted green,
To find once more the Suffolk he had known
Before the Somme. Yet there was not one tree
Unconscious of that name and aftermath
Nor is there now. For everything we see
Teaches the time that we are living in,
Whose piecemeal speech the vocables of Eden
Pace in reminder of the full perfection,
As oaks above these waters keep their gold
Against the autumn long past other trees
Poised between paradise and history.


# NIGHT FISHERS

After the autumn storms, we chose a night
    To fish the bay. The catch
I scarcely recollect. It was the climb,
    The grasp at slipping rock unnerved
All thought, thrust out of time
    And into now the sharp original fear
That mastered me then. I do not think
    I ever looked so far down into space
As through the clefts we over-leapt:
    Beams of our torches given back
Off walls and water in each rift
    Crossed and recrossed one another, so the mind
Recalling them, still seems to move
    Inside a hollow diamond that the dark
As shadows shift, threatens to unfacet:

It was no jewel, it was the flesh would shatter.
And yet it did not. Somehow we arrived
    And crouched there in the cool. The night
Save for the whispered water under-cliff,
    The hiss of falling casts, lay round
Thick with silence. It seemed
    A sky spread out beneath us, constellations
Swimming into view wherever fish
    Lit up its dark with phosphor. A thousand
Points of light mapped the expanse
    And depth, and yet the cliff-top height
Hinted no pull of vertigo along
    Its sudden edge: through diaphanous waters
The radium in the flowing pitchblende glowed
    Holding both mind and eye
Encompassed by a stir of scattered lambency:
    And unalarmed, I could forget
As night-bound we fished on unharmed,
    The terrors of the way we'd come, put by
The terrors of return past fault and fall,
    Watching this calm firmament of the sea.


# THE MOMENT


Watching two surfers walk toward the tide,
Floating their boards beside them as the shore
Drops slowly off, and first the knee, then waist
Goes down into the elemental grasp,
I look to them to choose it, as the one
Wave gathers itself from thousands and comes on:
And they are ready for it facing round
Like birds that turn to levitate in wind:
All is assured now as they slide abreast:
Much as I envy them their bodies' skill

To steady and prolong the wild descent,
I choose that moment when their choice agrees
And, poised, they hesitate as though in air
To a culmination half theirs and half the sea's.


## WRITING ON SAND

Birds' feet and baby feet,
Man Friday prints,
dog-pads
cramponned with claws,
ribbed shoe-soles—
hints there
of a refusal
to bare oneself
to the elemental,
a pacing parallel
to the incoming onrush, a
careful circuiting
of the rock pools:
the desire to stay
dry to be read
in the wet dust.
By what way
did that one
return?—he
of the stark striders,
the two perfect five-toed
concaves aimed
direct at the waves
whose own aim is
to remove
all clues
under the primeval slidings,

to erase them
to a swimming Braille,
an illegible Ogham,
to wash the slate clean.


# VALLE DE OAXACA

*for Roberto Donis*

Trumpeters
from the Comandancia militar
in the last glare of day
are practising a fanfare:

their notes float off
buffeted by walls
into a shower of chromatics
that falls round the ears of the women at the washing trough:

a celebration? You might call it that
as it harmonises with the tones
that toll from Santo Domingo—
a celebration, but of what?

Oh it's a desultory enough affair
I know: perhaps little more
than that the sun is shining
and they are standing where they are

under a tree's wide shade
where they've begun
to lay their instruments down
as they cross to the other side

of the barrack yard
to join the talkers there,
easy as unhurried men should be
conversing in the cooling air:

the abandoned instruments
gleam on, a heap
the low sun grazes
tracing the glinting contours of a sleep

tomorrow's dawn will scatter as
trumpeters set lips to brass
to waken also us as they
shake down reveilleing echoes over town and valley

# The Return (1987)

## IN THE BORGHESE GARDENS

*for Attilio Bertolucci*

Edging each other towards consummation
On the public grass and in the public eye,
Under the Borghese pines the lovers
Cannot tell what thunderheads mount the sky,
To mingle with the roar of afternoon
Rumours of the storm that must drench them soon.

Cars intersect the cardinal's great dream,
His parterres redesigned, gardens half-gone,
Yet Pluto's grasp still bruises Proserpine,
Apollo still hunts Daphne's flesh in stone,
Where the Borghese statuary and trees command
The ever-renewing city from their parkland.

The unbridled adolescences of gods
Had all of earth and air to cool their flights
And to rekindle. But where should lovers go
These torrid afternoons, these humid nights
While Daphne twists in leaves, Apollo burns
And Proserpine returns, returns, returns?

Rome is still Rome. Its ruins and its squares
Stand sluiced in wet and all its asphalt gleaming,
The street fronts caged behind the slant of rain-bars
Sun is already melting where they teem:
Spray-haloed traffic taints your laurel leaves,
City of restitutions, city of thieves.

Lovers, this giant hand, half-seen, sustains
By lifting up into its palm and plane
Our littleness: the shining causeway leads
Through arches, bridges, avenues and lanes
Of stone, that brought us first to this green place—
Expelled, we are the heirs of healing artifice.

Deserted now, and all that callow fire
Quenched in the downpour, here the parkland ways
Reach out into the density of dusk,
Between an Eden lost and promised paradise,
That overbrimming scent, rain-sharpened, fills,
Girdled within a rivercourse and seven hills.


## REVOLUTION
### PIAZZA DI SPAGNA

REVOLUTION it says
painted in purple along
the baluster of the Spanish
Steps and yes
you can return
by the other side
of this double stair
to where the word
is guiding you
(a little breathless)
down, up and back:
returning
you must run a ring
round the sun-browned
drop-outs
who litter the ascent:
their flights are inward

unlike these,
unfolding by degrees
what was once a hill,
each step a lip
of stone and what they say
to the sauntering eye
as clear as the day
they were made
to measure out and treasure
each rising inch
that nature had mislaid:
for only art
can return us to an Eden where
each plane and part
is bonded, fluid, fitting and
fits like this stair.


## FOUNTAIN


Art grows from hurt, you say. And I must own
Adam in Eden would have need of none.
Yet why should it not flow as a Roman fountain,
A fortunate fall between the sun and stone?
All a fountain can simulate and spread—
Scattering a music of public places
Through murmurs, mirrors, secrecy and shade—
Makes reparation for what hurt gave rise
To a wish to speak beyond the wound's one mouth,
And draw to singleness the several voices
That double a strength, diversify a truth,
Letting a shawl of water drape, escape
The basin's brim reshaping itself to fill
A whole clear cistern with its circling calm,
And the intricacies of moss and marble
With echoes of distance, aqueduct and hill.

# THE RETURN

*to Paolo Bertolani*

## I THE ROAD

I could not draw a map of it, this road,
Nor say with certainty how many times
It doubles on itself before it climbs
Clear of the ascent. And yet I know
Each bend and vista and could not mistake
The recognitions, the recurrences
As they occur, nor where. So my forgetting
Brings back the track of what was always there
As new as a discovery. And now
The summit gives us all that lies below,
Shows us the islands slide into their places
Beyond the shore and, when the lights come on,
How all the other roads declare themselves
Garlanding their gradients to the sea,
How the road that brought us here has dropped away
A half-lost contour on a chart of lights
The waters ripple and spread across the bay.

## II BETWEEN SERRA AND ROCCHETTA

Walking to La Rocchetta, thirty years
Would not be long enough to teach the mind
Flower by flower their names and their succession.
Walking to La Rocchetta, leave behind
The road, the fortress and the radar tower
And turn across the hill. From thirty years
I have brought back the image to the place.
The place has changed, the image still remains—
A spot that, niched above a half-seen bay,
Climbs up to catch the glitter from beyond

Of snow and marble off the Apennines.
But where are the walls, the wells, the living lines
That led the water down from plot to plot?
Hedges have reached the summits of the trees
Over the reeds and brambles no one cut.
When first I came, it was a time of storms:
Grey seas, uneasily marbling, scourged the cliff:
The waters had their way with skiff on skiff
And, beached, their sides were riven against stone,
Or, anchored, rode the onrush keels in air
Where hope and livelihood went down as one.
Two things we had in common, you and I
Besides our bitterness at want of use,
And these were poetry and poverty:
This was a place of poverty and splendour:
All unprepared, when clarity returned
I felt the sunlight prise me from myself
And from the youthful sickness I had learned
As shield from disappointments: cure came slow
And came, in part, from what I grew to know
Here on this coast among its reefs and islands.
I looked to them for courage across time,
Their substance shaped itself to mind and hand—
Severe the grace a place and people share
Along this slope where Serra took its stand:
For years I held those shapes in thought alone,
Certain you must have left long since, and then
Returning found that you had never gone.
What is a place? For you a single spot.
Walking to La Rocchetta we can trace
In all that meets the eye and all that does not
Half of its history, the other lies
In the rise, the run, the fall of voices:
Innumerable conversations chafe the air
At thresholds and in alleys, street and square
Of those who climbed this slope to work its soil,
And phrases marrying a tongue and time

Coil through the mind's ear, climbing now with us
Through orchids and the wild asparagus:
For place is always an embodiment
And incarnation beyond argument,
Centre and source where altars, once, would rise
To celebrate those lesser deities
We still believe in—angels beyond fable
Who still might visit the patriarch's tent and table
Both here and now, or rather let us say
They rustle through the pages you and I
Rooted in earth, have dedicated to them.
Under the vines the fireflies are returning:
Pasolini spoke of their extinction.
Our lookout lies above a poisoned sea:
Wrong, he was right, you tell us—I agree,
Of one thing the enigma is quite sure,
We have lived into a time we shall not cure.
But climbing to La Rocchetta, let there be
One sole regret to cross our path today,
That she, who tempered your beginning pen
Will never take this road with us again
Or hear, now, the full gamut of your mastery.


### III GRAZIELLA

We cannot climb these slopes without our dead;
We need no fiction of a hillside ghosted,
A fade-out on the tremor of the sea.
The dead do not return, and nor shall we
To pry and prompt the living or rehearse
The luxuries of self-debating verse.
Their silence we inhabit now they've gone
And like a garment drawn the darkness on
Beyond all hurt. This quiet we must bear:
Put words into their mouths, you fail to hear
What once they said. I can recall the day
She imitated my clipped, foreign way

Of saying *Shakespeare*: English, long unheard,
Came flying back, some unfamiliar bird
Cutting a wing-gust through the weight of air
As she repeated it—*Shakespeare Shakespeare*—
Voice-prints of a season that belongs
To the cicadas and the heat, their song
Shrill, simmering and continuous.
Why does a mere word seem autonomous
We catch back from the grave? The wave it rides
Was spent long-since, dissolved within the tides
Of space and time. And yet the living tone
Shaped to that sound, and mocking at its own,
A voice at play, amused, embodied, clear,
Spryer than any ghost still haunts the ear.
The dog days, the cicada had returned
And through that body more than summer burned
A way and waste into its dark terrain,
Burned back and back till nothing should remain,
Yet could not dry the mind up at its source:
Clear as her voice-print, its unyielded force
Would not be shadowed out of clarity
Until the moment it had ceased to be.
Downhill, between the olives, more than eye
Must tell the foot what path it travels by;
The sea-lights' constellations sway beneath
And we are on the Easter side of death.


## IV THE FIREFLIES

I have climbed blind the way down through the trees
(How faint the phosphorescence of the stones)
On nights when not a light showed on the bay
And nothing marked the line of sky and sea—
Only the beating of the heart defined
A space of being in the faceless dark,

The foot that found and won the path from blindness,
The hand, outstretched, that touched on branch and bark.
The soundless revolution of the stars
Brings back the fireflies and each constellation,
And we are here half-shielded from that height
Whose star-points feed the white lactation, far
Incandescence where the single star
Is lost to sight. This is a waiting time.
Those thirty, lived-out years were slow to rhyme
With consonances unforeseen, and, gone,
Were brief beneath the seasons and the sun.
We wait now on the absence of our dead,
Sharing the middle world of moving lights
Where fireflies taking torches to the rose
Hover at those clustered, half-lit porches,
Eyelid on closed eyelid in their glow
Flushed into flesh, then darkening as they go.
The adagio of lights is gathering
Across the sway and counter-lines as bay
And sky, contrary in motion, swerve
Against each other's patternings, while these
Tiny, travelling fires gainsay them both,
Trusting to neither empty space nor seas
The burden of their weightless circlings. We,
Knowing no more of death than other men
Who make the last submission and return,
Savour the good wine of a summer's night
Fronting the islands and the harbour bar,
Uncounted in the sum of our unknowings
How sweet the fireflies' span to those who live it,
Equal, in their arrivals and their goings,
With the order and the beauty of star on star.

# CATACOMB

A capuchin—long acquaintance with the dead
   Has left him taciturn—stands guard
At gate and stairhead. Silent, he awaits
   The coin we drop into his dish, and then
Withdraws to contemplation—though his eye
   Glides with a marvellous economy sideways
Towards the stair, in silent intimation
   *You may now descend*. We do—and end up
In a corridor with no end in view: dead
   Line the perspective left and right
Costumed for resurrection. The guidebook had not lied
   Or tidied the sight away—and yet
*Eight thousand* said, unseen, could scarcely mean
   The silence throughout this city of the dead,
Street on street of it calling into question
   That solidity the embalmer would counterfeit.
Mob-cap, cape, lace, stole and cowl,
   Frocked children still at play
In the Elysian fields of yesterday
   Greet each morning with a morning face
Put on a century ago. Why are we here?—
   Following this procession, bier on bier
(The windowed dead, within), and those
   Upright and about to go, but caught
Forever in their parting pose, as though
   They might have died out walking. Some
Face us from the wall, like damaged portraits;
   Some, whose clothing has kept its gloss,
Glow down across the years at us
   *Why are you here?* And why, indeed,
For the sunlight through a lunette overhead
   Brightens along a sinuous bole of palm:
Leaves catch and flare it into staring green
   Where a twine of tendril sways inside

Between the bars. Light from that sky
    Comes burning off the bay
Vibrant with Africa; in public gardens
    Tenses against the butterflies' descent
The stamens of red hibiscus. Dead
    Dressed for the promenade they did not take,
Are leaning to that light: it is the sun
    Must judge them, for the sin
Of vanity sits lightly on them: it is the desire
    To feel its warmth against the skin
Has set them afoot once more in this parade
    Of epaulette, cockade and crinoline. We are here
Where no northern measure can undo
    So single-minded a lure—if once a year
The house of the dead stood open
    And these, dwelling beneath its roof,
Were shown the world's great wonders,
    They would marvel beyond every other thing
At the sun. Today, the dead
    Look out from their dark at us
And keep their counsel. The capuchin
    Has gone off guard, to be replaced
By a brother sentry whose mind is elsewhere—
    Averted from this populace whose conversion
Was nominal after all. His book
    Holds fast his eyes from us. His disregard
Abolishes us as we pass beyond the door.

                                        *Palermo*

157

# THE MIRACLE OF THE BOTTLE
# AND THE FISHES

## I

What is it Braque
would have us see in this
piled-up table-top of his?

One might even take it for
a cliff-side, sky-high
accumulation opening door on door

of space. We do not know
with precision or at a glance
which is space and which is substance,

nor should we yet: the eye must stitch
each half-seen, separate
identity together

in a mind delighted and disordered by
a freshness of the world's own weather.

## II

To enter space anew:
to enter a new space
inch by inch and not
the perspective avenue
cutting a swathe through mastered distance
from a viewpoint that is single:
'If you painted nothing but profiles
you would grow to believe
men have only one eye.'
Touch must supply
space with its substance and become
a material of the exploration

as palpable as paint,
in a reciprocation where
things no longer stand
bounded by emptiness: 'I begin,'
he says, 'with the background
that supports the picture
like the foundation of a house.'


### III

These layered darknesses
project no image of a mind
in collusion with its spectres:
in this debate
of shadow and illumination fate
does not hang heavily
over an uncertain year
(it is nineteen-twelve) for the eye
leaves fate undone
refusing to travel straitened
by either mood or taken measure:
it must stumble, it must touch
to guess how much of space
for all its wilderness
is both honeycomb and home.


## IN MEMORY OF GEORGE OPPEN


We were talking of O'Hara.
'Difficult', you said
'to imagine a good death—*he died
quietly in bed*, in place of:
*he was run down
by a drunk*.' And now, your own.
First, the long unskeining year by year

of memory and mind. You 'seemed
to be happy' is all I hear.
A lost self does not hide:
what seemed happy was not you
who died before you died. And yet
out of nonentity, where did the words
spring from when
towards the end you told
your sister, 'I don't know
if you have anything to say
but let's take out all the adjectives
and we'll find out'—the way,
lucidly unceremonious,
you spoke to her in life and us.


## THE TAX INSPECTOR

*at Tlacolula*

I had been here before.
I came back
to see the chapel
of hacked saints.
It was shut.
A funeral filled
the body of the church:
small women with vast lilies
heard out the mass: the priest
completing communion
wiped wine
from his lips and from
the gold chalice
which having dried
he disposed of: the event
was closed. The organ
whose punctuations

had accompanied the rite
broke into a waltz
and the women
rose and the *compañeros*
*de trabajo* of the dead man
shouldered the coffin forth
to daylight. The waltz
seemed right as did
the deathmarch, the woe
of the inconsolable brass
preceding to the *campo santo*
the corpse, the women
and the *compañeros*
who sweated from street to street
under the bier,
swaying it like a boat.
And this was the way—
a banner declaring
what work he and his *compañeros*
had once shared—
the tax inspector,
ferried across on human flesh,
was borne to burial.

## *from* 'Winter Journey'

When you wrote to tell of your arrival,
　　It was midnight, you said, and knew
In wishing me *Goodnight* that I
　　Would have been long abed. And that was true.
I was dreaming your way for you, my dear,
　　Freed of the mist that followed the snow here,
And yet it followed you (within my dream, at least)
　　Nor could I close my dreaming eye
To the thought of further snow
　　Widening the landscape as it sought
The planes and ledges of your moorland drive.
　　I saw a scene climb up around you
That whiteness had marked out and multiplied
　　With a thousand touches beyond the green
And calculable expectations summer in such a place
　　Might breed in one. My eye took in
Close-to, among the vastnesses you passed unharmed,
　　The shapes the frozen haze hung on the furze
Like scattered necklaces the frost had caught
　　Half-unthreaded in their fall. It must have been
The firm prints of your midnight pen
　　Over my fantasia of snow, told you were safe,
Turning the threats from near and far
　　To images of beauty we might share
As we shared my dream that now
　　Flowed to the guiding motion of your hand,
As though through the silence of propitious dark
　　It had reached out to touch me across sleeping England.

# A ROSE FOR JANET

I know
this rose is only
an ink-and-paper rose
but see how it grows and goes
on growing
beneath your eyes:
a rose in flower
has had (almost) its vegetable hour
whilst my
rose of spaces and typography
can reappear at will
(your will)
whenever you repeat
this ceremony of the eye
from the beginning
and thus
learn how
to resurrect a rose
that's instantaneous
perennial
and perfect now

# THE WELL

*for Norman Nicholson*

We loosen the coping-stone that has sealed for years
    The mid-field well. We slide-off this roof
That has taken root. We cannot tell
    How the single, pale tendril of ivy
Has trailed inside nor where
    In the dark it ends. Past the dark
A small, clear mirror sends
    Our images back to us, the trees
Framing the roundel that we make,
    A circling frieze that answers to the form
Of this tunnel, coiled cool in brick.
    We let down the plumbline we have improvised
Out of twine and a stone, and as it arrives,
    Sounding and sounding past round on round of wall,
Our images liquidly multiply, flow out
    And past all bounds to drown in the dazzle
As a laugh of light runs echoing up from below.


# THE HAWTHORN IN TRENT VALE

After fifty years, the hawthorn hedge
    That ran through the new estate
Still divides the garden ends, resists
    With wounds to wrist and elbow every move
To fell it or constrain. This ghost
    From a farm now gone, remains to haunt
And prick the sleep of gardeners dreaming ill
    Of the one unaccommodating dendrophil
Who has tenderly let his portion swell into tree entire,
    Green fire and blossom fed
From the darkness under bed and masonry.

# ARARAT

We shall sleep-out together through the dark
The earth's slow voyage across centuries
Towards whatever Ararat its ark
Is steering for. Our atoms then will feel
The jarring and arrival of that keel
In timelessness, and rise through galaxies,
Motes starred by the first and final light to show
Whether those shores are habitable or no.

# *Annunciations* (1989)

## ANNUNCIATION

The cat took fright
at the flashing wing of sunlight
as the thing
entered the kitchen, angel of appearances,
and lingered there.

What was it the sun
had sent to say
by his messenger, this solvent ray,
that charged and changed
all it looked at, narrowing even the eye of a cat?

Utensils caught a shine
that could not be used, utility
unsaid by this invasion
from outer space, this gratuitous occasion
of unchaptered gospel.

'I shall return,' the appearance promised,
'I shall not wait for the last
day—every day
is fortunate even when you catch
my ray only as a gliding ghost.

What I foretell
is the unaccountable birth each time
my lord the light, a cat and you
share this domestic miracle:
it asks the name anew

of each thing named
when an earlier, shining dispensation
reached down into mist
and found the solidity
these windows and these walls surround,

and where each cup,
dish, hook and nail
now gathers and guards the sheen
drop by drop
still spilling-over
out of the grail of origin.'


## THE BLADE


I looked to the west:
I saw it thrust
a single blade
between the shadows:
a lean stiletto-shard
tapering to its tip
yellowed along greensward,
lit on a roof that lay
mid-way across its path
and then outran it:
it was so keen,
it seemed to go
right through and cut
in two the land
it was lancing. Then
as I stood,
the shaft shifted,
fading across grass,
withdrew as visibly as the sand
down the throat of an hour-glass:

you could see time
trickle out, a grainy
lesion, and the green
filter back to fill
the crack in creation.


## ABOVE THE RIO GRANDE

*for Claude-Marie Senninger*

The light, in its daylong play, refuses
    The mountains' certainty that they
Will never change—range on range of them
    In an illumination that looks like snow.
On this afternoon when the clouds are one impending grey
    Above the Rio Grande, the light will not obey
Either the clouds' or the rocks' command
    To keep its distance from them. It shifts and shows
Even the cloudshadows how to transform
    The very stones by opening over them
Dark wings that cradle and crease their solidity—
    As if to say: I gather up the rocks
Out of their world of things that are merely things,
    I call dark wings to be bearers of light
As they sail off the shapes they pall
    And, in their wake, leave this brightening snowfall
That melts and is renewed. Yet if the light
    Washes the rocks away, the rocks remain
To tell what it is, and only so
    Can they both flow and stay, and the mind
That floating thing, steady to know itself
    In all the exceedings of its certainty,
As here, beneath the expanses deepening
    Through the cloud-rock ranges of evening sky.

# THE PLAZA

People are the plot
and what they do here—
which is mostly sit
or walk through. The afternoon sun
brings out the hornets:
they dispute with no one, they too
are enjoying their ease
along the wet brink of the fountain,
imbibing peace and water
until a child arrives,
takes off his shoe
and proceeds methodically
to slaughter them. He has the face
and the ferocious concentration
of one of those Aztec gods
who must be fed on blood.
His mother drags him away, half-shod,
and then puts back the shoe
over a dusty sock.
Some feet go bare, some sandalled,
like these Indians who march through
—four of them—carrying a bed
as if they intended to sleep here.
Their progress is more brisk
than that of the ants at our feet
who are removing—some
by its feelers, some
supporting it on their backs—
a dead moth
as large as a bird.
As the shadows densen
in the gazebo-shaped bandstand
the band are beginning to congregate.
The air would be tropical
but for the breath of the sierra:

it grows opulent on the odour
of jacaranda and the turpentine
of the shoeshine boys
busy at ground-level,
the squeak of their rags on leather
like an angry, repeated bird-sound.
The conductor rises,
flicks his score with his baton—
moths are circling the bandstand light—
and sits down after each item.
The light falls onto the pancakes
of the flat military hats
that tilt and nod
as the musicians under them
converse with one another—then,
the tap of the baton. It must be
the presence of so many flowers enriches the brass:
tangos take on a tragic air,
but the opaque scent
makes the modulation into waltz-time seem
an invitation—not to the waltz merely—
but to the thought that there may be
the choice (at least for the hour)
of dying like Carmen
then rising like a flower.
A man goes by, carrying a fish
that is half his length
wrapped in a sheet of plastic
but nobody sees him. And nobody hears
the child in a torn dress
selling artificial flowers,
mouthing softly in English, 'Flowerrs'.
High heels, bare feet
around the tin cupola of the bandstand
patrol to the beat of the band:
this is the democracy
of the tierra templada—a contradiction
in a people who have inherited

so much punctilio, and yet
in all the to-and-fro
there is no frontier set:
the shopkeepers, the governor's sons,
the man who is selling balloons
in the shape of octopuses, bandannaed heads
above shawled and suckled children
keep common space
with a trio of deaf mutes
talking together in signs,
all drawn to the stir
of this rhythmic pulse
they cannot hear. The musicians
are packing away their instruments:
the strollers have not said out their say
and continue to process
under the centennial trees.
A moon has worked itself free
of the excluding boughs
above the square, and stands
unmistily mid-sky, a precisionist.
The ants must have devoured their prey by this.
As for the fish . . . three surly Oaxaqueños
are cutting and cooking it
to feed a party of French-speaking Swiss
at the Hotel Calesa Real.
The hornets that failed to return
stain the fountain's edge,
the waters washing and washing away at them,
continuing throughout the night
their whisperings of ablution
where no one stirs,
to the shut flowerheads and the profuse stars.

*Oaxaca*

# FAR POINT

*(British Columbia)*

The road ends here. If your way
lies north, then you must take
to the forest or the bay. A café
which is a poolroom which is a bar
serves clams and beer;
the woman who brings them in,
a cheerful exile here,
counts out coins
'Eins, zwei, drei . . .'
with the queen's head on them.
'Look!' I hear her say: a skiff
with an outboard goes past the window.
It's from the island (a strip of sand
with pines and houses on it) and a deer
is swimming in its wake. 'It belongs
to the people in the boat. They should mark it.
I knew a couple who tamed a seal.
It would swim behind *them*, too,
then one day somebody shot it.'
'How would you mark a seal?' I say . . .
'It's easy to mark a deer.
You know how he found it?
It was being born. Out in the woods.
He couldn't resist touching the fur
so the mother abandoned it—
it was the smell of a man on it frightened her.'
The man opens the door:
a group of Indians are playing pool,
the usual clientele on the bar stools.
They look like lumberjacks. Americans,
they came north to stay out of the army
and never went back. Now they are grey.
He joins them and the deer
paces the veranda and tries

172

with its great deer's eyes
to look through
the deceptions of the long window
and find where he is.
The pool-players, backs to the light,
stand facing away
from centuries of clambake, potlatch
and tribal ferocities
down a totem-guarded coast.
The poles rotted and the seeds,
dropping inside their crevices,
turned them back into trees.
The cue's click, click
rehearses its softly merciless music
ticking away the increment
of unwanted time. We return
to the car, past fragile shacks
whose cracked white paint
the sea air is picking apart.
We discover the deer once more
that gazes right through us,
then catching sight of a pair of dogs
arcs off to play with them,
perhaps thinks it's a dog.
Across the blue-grey strait,
the ragged ideograms of firs
in a rising and falling fog:
clouds are what we appear to contemplate
above them, then the mist
stirs, sails off
and we see it is summits
we are peering at,
that go on unveiling themselves
as if they were being created.

# CARRARA REVISITED

Only in flight could you gather at a glance
So much of space and depth as from this height;
Yet flight would blur the unbroken separation
Of fragile sounds from solid soundlessness—
The chime of metal against distant stone,
The crumple and the crumble of devastation
Those quarries filter up at us. Our steps,
As they echo on this marble mountain,
Make us seem gods whom that activity
Teems to placate. But not for long. The hawk
Stretched on the air is more a god than we,
And sees us from above as our eyes see
The minute and marble-heavy trucks that sway
Slowly across the sheernesses beneath us, bend on bend,
Specks on an endlessly descending causeway.


# THE HOUSE IN THE QUARRY

What is it doing there, this house in the quarry?
    On the scrap of a height it stands its ground:
The cut-away cliffs rise round it
    And the dust lies heavy along its sills.
Still lived in? It must be, with the care
    They have taken to train its vine
Whose dusty pergola keeps back the blaze
    From a square of garden. Can it be melons
They are growing, a table someone has set out there
    As though, come evening, you might even sit at it
Drinking wine? What dusty grapes
    Will those writhen vine-stocks show for the rain
To cleanse in autumn? And will they taste then
    Of the lime-dust of this towering waste,

174

Or have transmuted it to some sweetness unforeseen
	That original cleanliness could never reach
Rounding to insipidity? All things
	Seem possible in this unreal light—
The poem still to be quarried here,
	The house itself lit up to repossess
Its stolen site, as the evening matches
	Quiet to the slowly receding thunder of the last
Of the lorries trundling the unshaped marble down and past.


## AT THE AUTUMN EQUINOX

*for Giuseppe Conte*

Wild boars come down by night
	Sweet-toothed to squander a harvest
In the vines, tearing apart
	The careful terraces whose clinging twines
Thicken out to trunks and seem
	To hold up the pergolas they embrace.
Make fast the gate. Under a late moon
	That left the whole scene wild and clear,
I came on twenty beasts, uprooting, browsing
	Here these ledges let into the hillside.
They had undone and taken back again
	Into their nomad scavengers' domain
All we had shaped for use, and laid it waste
	In a night's carouse. Which story is true?
Those who are not hunters say that hunters brought
	The beasts to this place, to multiply for sport
And that they bred here, spread. Or should one credit
	The tale told of that legendary winter
A century since, which drove them in starving bands
	Out from the frozen heartlands of the north?

Ice had scabbed every plane and pine,
    Tubers and roots lay slabbed beneath the ground
That nothing alive or growing showed above
    To give promise of subsistence. They drove on still
Until they found thickets greening up through snow
    And ate the frozen berries from them. Then
Down to the lowland orchards and the fields
    Where crops rooted and ripened. Or should one
Go back to beginnings and to when
    No men had terraced out these slopes? Trees
Taller than the oaks infested then
    These rocks now barren, their lianas
Reaching to the shore—the shore whose miles
    On miles of sand saw the first approach
As swarms swam inland from the isles beyond
    And took possession. Are these
The remnant of that horde, forsaking forests
    And scenting the orchards in their wake? I could hear them
Crunch and crush a whole harvest
    From the vines while the moon looked on.
A mouse can ride on a boar's back,
    Nest in its fur, gnaw through the hide and fat
And not disturb it, so obtuse is their sense of touch—
    But not of sight or smell. I stood
Downwind and waited. It takes five dogs
    To hunt a boar. I had no gun
Nor, come to that, the art to use one:
    I was man alone: I had no need
Of legends to assure me how strange they were—
    A sufficiency of fear confessed their otherness.
*Stay still* I heard the heartbeats say:
    I could see all too clear
In the hallucinatory moonlight what was there.
    Day led them on. Next morning found
These foragers on ground less certain
    Than dug soil or the gravel-beds
Of dried-up torrents. Asphalt
    Confused their travelling itch, bemused

And drew them towards the human outskirts.
    They clattered across its too-smooth surfaces—
Too smooth, yet too hard for those snouts
    To root at, or tusks to tear out
The rootage under it. Its colour and its smell,
    The too-sharp sunlight, the too-tepid air
Stupefied the entire band: water
    That they could swim, snow that had buried
All sustenance from them, worried them far less
    Than this man-made ribbon luring them on
Helpless into the shadow of habitation.
    The first building at the entrance to the valley
Had *Carabinieri* written across its wall:
    Challenged, the machine-gunned law
Saw to it with one raking volley
    And brought the procession to the ground,
Then sprayed it again, to put beyond all doubt
    That this twitching confusion was mostly dead
And that the survivors should not break out
    Tusked and purposeful to defend themselves.
Blood on the road. A crowd, curious
    To view the end of this casual hecatomb
And lingeringly inspect what a bullet can do.
    It was like the conclusion of all battles.
Who was to be pitied and who praised?
    Above the voices, the air hung
Silent, cleared, by the shots, of birdsong
    And as torn into, it seemed, as the flesh below.
Quietly now, at the edges of the crowd,
    Hunters looked the disdain they felt
For so unclean a finish, and admired
    The form those backs, subdued, still have,
Lithe as the undulation of a wave. The enemy
    They had seen eviscerate a dog with a single blow
Brought into the thoughts of these hunters now
    Only their poachers' bitterness at flesh foregone
As their impatience waited to seize on the open season,
    The autumn equinox reddening through the trees.

# THE BUTTERFLIES

They cover the tree and twitch their coloured capes,
   On thin legs, stalking delicately across
The blossoms breathing nectar at them;
   Hang upside-down like bats,
Like wobbling fans, stepping, tipping,
   Tipsily absorbed in what they seek and suck.
There is a bark-like darkness
   Of patterned wrinklings as though of wood
As wings shut against each other.
   Folded upon itself, a black
Cut-out has quit the dance;
   One opens, closes from splendour into drab,
Intent antennae preceding its advance
   Over a floor of flowers. Their skeletons
Are all outside—fine nervures
   Tracing the fourfold wings like leaves;
Their mouths are for biting with—they breathe
   Through stigmata that only a lens can reach:
The faceted eyes, a multiplying glass
   Whose intricacies only a glass can teach,
See us as shadows if they see at all.
   It is the beauty of wings that reconciles us
To these spindles, angles, these inhuman heads
   Dipping and dipping as they sip.
The dancer's tread, the turn, the pirouette
   Come of a choreography not ours,
Velvets shaken out over flowers on flowers
   That under a thousand (can they be felt as) feet
Dreamlessly nod in vegetative sleep.

# HARVEST

*for Paula and Fred*

After the hay was baled and stacked in henges,
We walked through the circles in the moonlit field:
The moon was hidden from us by the ranges
Of hills that enclosed the meadows hay had filled.

But its light lay one suffusing undertone
That drew out the day and changed the pace of time:
It slowed to the pulse of our passing feet upon
Gleanings the baler had left on the ground to rhyme

With the colour of the silhouettes that arose,
Dark like the guardians of a frontier strayed across,
Into this in-between of time composed —
Sentries of Avalon, these megaliths of grass.

Yet it was time that brought us to this place,
Time that had ripened the grasses harvested here:
Time will tell us tomorrow that we paced
Last night in a field that is no longer there.

And yet it was. And time, the literalist,
The sense and the scent of it woven in time's changes,
Cannot put by that sweetness, that persistence
After the hay was baled and stacked in henges.


# LETTER TO UEHATA

Since I returned, the trees have a Japanese look,
    And bare in their wintry sinuousness seem
To retrace in air the windings of those paths
    That followed so faithfully the swelling ground,

179

Then lost for an instant, came back into view
    With the trees they wound on through, reflected
(Borrowed, as you would say) by some pool.
    That landscape was arranged—to reflect
And reflect again the grain and grandeur
    Of the world we see, and that the centuries
Have unrolled to now, as if time
    Were itself the paradigm of a path
That has brought me to where I can read
    In the bareness of the trees a double scene—
Where I am now and where we both were then.


## ORION OVER FARNE

*for John Casken*


The growling of the constellations, you said—
    A more ferocious music of the spheres
Where, above Farne, the Scorpion tears
    Orion still, teaches him hunt elsewhere,
But hunt he will—and here
    Over the breathing body of the sea,
Heard through the darkness and the star-rimed air
    To the sharp percussions of the tide on scree.
Close to, a poet feeds this frosty soil
    Where the November constellation sets
As storms on storms begin, as the spoils
    Of another year are scattered and constellation
On hunted constellation grinds and growls.

# CHANCE

I saw it as driving snow, the spume,
    Then, as the waves hit rock
Foam-motes took off like tiny birds
    Drawn downwind in their thousands
Coiled in its vortices. They settled
    Along ledges and then fell back,
Condensed on the instant at the touch of stone
    And slid off, slicking the rock-sides
As they went. The tide went, too,
    Dragging the clicking pebbles with it
In a cast of chattering dice. What do they tell
    These occurrences, these resemblances that speak to you
With no human voice? What they told then
    Was that the energies pouring through space and time,
Spun into snow-lace, suspended into flight
    Had waited on our chance appearance here,
To take their measure, to re-murmur in human sounds
    The nearing roar of this story of far beginnings
As it shapes out and resounds itself along the shore.


# THE HEADLAND

A silence lies over the headland like a death
    That has left in the air an echo of the stir
That it has checked—you hear it in the breathing of the sea
    Lipping at the pebbles continuously
Below the cliff, as if it could not articulate
    The word it wanted to deliver, yet bringing to bear
All of the forces it takes to shape one word:
    Unseizably it rehearses an after-life
(The only one certainly there) like that of verse
    That holds its shell to the ear of a living man,

Reminding him that he will be outlasted
By the scansion in its waves, beating a shore
That is the beginning of the voyage out
Towards the continuing sunsets, on and on
Cast back across the façades of the shoreline town.


## FOR A GODCHILD

Given a godchild,
I must find a god
worthy of her. Dante
refused—in courtesy
(he said) to the god
he venerated, to wipe
a sinner's eyes in hell:
I must tell her of that
one day, and see
that she ponders well
what she takes to be
the dues of deity—
and learn that a god
who harbours anger where
thirst has no slaking,
eyes no ease,
is either of her own
or others' making.

# *The Door in the Wall* (1992)

## THE OPERATION

A cold spring morning sees
    The man who has come to trim trees
In the valley wood, up against a sky
    That looks down, through and into
A cat's cradle of twigs and branches.
    The man paces this swaying cage,
Giving thought to the size and shape
    Of what he must do, exploring
Floor by floor each pliant storey
    Threatened by rot and over-crowding:
He weighs by eye what high limbs
    Stand to fall, when winter squalls
Rake the valley, and rounds out
    His loppings to please the tidy mind
Of the owner of these trees. Then
    Into action: standing there
Forks apart, spanning half a branch,
    He power-saws the other half off
And scaling a stair of boughs, repeats
    At each rung his noisy squaring.
But what finesse—raucousness apart
    As the blade combusts—in the way that he
Slices the slender outgrowths from the tree,
    Works at it with a dabbing motion,
Then leans back, inspects and jabs again—
    Painting not pruning: he is as much
Making a tree as taking a tree apart,
    Walking a world of his own creation.

He darts with his saw, having at what he sees
     Like a slightly clumsy fencer. No—
'Clumsy' cannot be just. Who'd dare
     Fence on a beech bough, trust
To sprung pliancy fifty feet and more
     In air? A voice-over—caught
Between bursts from the ignited saw,
     Prompting *More to the right, more*
*To the road side*—proceeds from the critic
     (The artist heeds him, too) who lies
Stretched across the cab-roof of a truck
     Sizing up the shape of the new
Treescape after the morning's abbreviations:
     *That'll do*. The expert in metamorphoses
Restrains his saw, and leans
     Down into the twiggery to extricate
Boughs that have lodged in there,
     Tosses them to the ground with a crackling roar.
The painter and the fencer now disappear:
     He has one more image to dance
In and out of, and clings to his rope
     As a 'Me Tarzan' swing returns him
To the top of his ladder: he trots down,
     Hopping earthwards from five feet up
And walks horizontally away—primate
     Into man—to put a distance between
Himself and what he has done, and to survey it:
     The hard hat he appeared to be wearing
Turns out to be his own red hair.
     Then the corpse on the cab-roof
Suddenly resurrects: *Not bad*.
     His eyes—he is grounded, too—take in
The fallen logs they must soon begin
     Piling aboard and the litter along the road
To be gathered and fired, before moving on
     Down the freshly tarred approaches. Evening:

And the procession of their fires dies back
    To heaps of glowing ash, and a low haze
Starts climbing throughout the trees,
    Altering, as it flows into the twilight,
The million burin strokes of branches
    To soft charcoal lines, the incense
Leaving the senses open to the night.


## SIENA IN SIXTY-EIGHT


The town band, swaying dreamily on its feet,
    Under the portraits of Gramsci and Ho,
Play 'Selections from *Norma*', and the moon,
    Casta diva, mounts up to show
How high the sky is over harvested Tuscany,
    Over this communist conviviality within the wall
Of a fortress that defends nothing at all.

History turns to statues, to fancy dress
    And the stylishness of Guevara in his bonnet. Here,
Red-bloused, forgetful sales girls
    For the revolution, flirt with the males
At a bookstore under an awning of red:
    Lenin, Che, Debray and Mao—
The unbought titles, pristinely serried.

'Realism and sobriety' one might write of the art show:
    In *No to Repression*, a procession of women
With raised fists, shouts No, No, No.
    And between *American Bombers* and *Black Boy Cleaning Shoes*,
Somebody, unteachably out of step,
    Has gouged intently into paint
The stigmata of St Francis in *Miracle of the Saint*.

Consciences drowse this summer night
    Warmed by the after-glow. Fragrance of cooking
Weighs on the sense already fed by it,
    The wild boar turning and turning on its spit;
And the air too greasily replete to lift the red flag,
    The morning headlines grow fainter in the dusk:
'Where is Dubcek?' 'Tanks on the streets of Prague.'


## PARIS IN SIXTY-NINE

*for Octavio Paz*

'I love', I heard you say,
    'To walk in the morning.' We were walking,
Spring light sharpening each vista,
    Under the symmetrical, freshly-leafing trees,
By boulevard, bridge and quays the Douanier
    Had painted into his golden age
Of a Tour Eiffel perpetually new.
    I replied: 'I trust the thoughts that come to me
When walking. Do you, too, *work* when walking?'
    'Work when I am working . . . ?' My error
(Traffic was too loud to fight with words)
    Came clear to me at last—for I
Am far too fast imagining that my friends
    Prefer, like me, the stir of street or landscape
To four walls to work in. Sunlight
    Had begun, after a night of frost, to warm
The April air to temperate perfection,
    In which the mathematics of sharp shade
Would have gratified Le Nôtre, 'auteur de ce jardin':
    His bust surveyed it: in the pavilion there
The subtler geometries of Cézanne. Refaire
    Poussin après la nature!—he and the auteur
Might have seen eye to eye, perhaps
    But for the straight lines and the grandeur.

All was not easy here. Gendarmerie
    Clustered at corners, still unrelenting
After the late events, although the theatre
    Deserted by its actors now, lay silent
But for the sloganned walls. 'De Gaulle', I said,
    'Is an unpleasant man.' 'But a great one,'
You replied, to my surprise, for you
    Believed when the students had their Day
It was a sign that linearity
    Was coming to its close, and time
Was circling back to recurrence and fiesta.
    Before the walker the horizon slips from sight.
What matters in the end (it never comes)
    Is what is seen along the way.
Our feet now found confronting us
    The equestrian bulk ('Paris vaut une messe!')
Of Henri quatre in the Place Dauphine,
    Horsed on the spot that Breton called
'The sex of Paris', legs of roadways
    Straddling out from it. Was it the image
Drew him to that statue, or had he
    (Eros apart) a taste for monarchy?
'Pope of surrealism' is unfair, no doubt,
    And yet, it comprehends the way he chose
To issue edicts, excommunicate his friends.
    I saw his face look out from yours—
Or so it seemed—the day that I declined
    To dine in company, which led you on to say:
'Always the Englishman, you want to found
    *Another* church.' So, always the Englishman,
I compromised and came—Paris vaut une messe.
    For it was Paris held us on its palm,
Paris I was refusing as well as you
    And should have said no to neither:
Paris looked in on all we were to say and do,
    And every afternoon concluded with
That secular and urban miracle
    When the lights come on, not one by one,

But all at once, and the idea and actuality
    Of the place imprinted themselves on dusk,
Opening spaces undeclared by day.
    All the recurrences of that constellation
Never reunited us by that river.
    Yet, time finding us once more together
On English soil, has set us talking,
    So let me renew my unrequited question
From twenty years ago: 'Do you, Octavio,
    Work when you are walking . . . ?'


BLAUBEUREN


And now the season climbs in conflagration
    Up to the summits. The thick leaves
Glow on either side of the descent
    A fire-ride carves between the trees—
A blue, unsoundable abyss. The sun
    Is pushing upwards, firing into incandescence
Lingering vapours. The tufted pinetips
    Begin to define the hilltop where a cross—
Too blatant to beckon a heart towards it—
    Stands stolid and ghostly, a dogmatic
Concrete post hardening out of mist,
    And, grey to gold, touch by touch,
The wood mass—beams breaking in—
    Visibly looms above the town. Below
Floats back a climbing bell-chime
    Out of the theological centuries: that, too,
Caught up into the burning vibrancy,
    Seems yet another surface for refraction,
Fragmenting into audible tips of flame.
    The beacon of the day—the mist has burned away now—
Blazes towards the death and resurrection
    Of the year. To be outlived by this,

By the recurrences and the generations, as today
    Has lived beyond the century of Dürer—
His rocks stand jutting from the foliage here—
    Is to say: I have lived
Between the red blaze and the white,
    I have taken the sacrament of the leaf
That spells my death, and I have asked to be,
    Breathing it in at every pore of sense,
Servant to all I see riding this wave
    Of fire and air—the circling hawk,
The leaves . . . no, they are butterflies
    That love the ash like leaves and then
Come dancing down from it, all lightness
    And away. Lord, make us light enough
To bear the message of this fine flame
    Rising off rooted things, and render it
Back to the earth beneath them, turning earth
    Itself, while the light still holds,
To a steady burning, a clarity
    Bordering the blue, deep fold of shadow:
Cars, weaving the woodslope road,
    Glitter like needles through the layered leaves.


## THE DOOR IN THE WALL

*i.m. Jorge Guillén*


Under the door in the wall
the slit of sun
pours out at the threshold
such an illumination,

one begins to picture
the garden in there,
making the wrinkled step
seem shadowy, bare;

but within the shadows
an underfoot world puts forth
in points of light
its facets of worth—

surfaces of such depth
you have only to eye them,
to find you are travelling
a constellation by them;

and the sun that whitens
every lightward plane
leaks up the stone jamb,
reappears again

where the flickering tangle
of thick leaves cover
the top of the wall and
ivy piles over.

So the garden in there
cannot mean merely
an ornamental perfection
when the gardener lets be

this climbing parasite
within whose folds
birds find a shelter
against rain and cold.

But let be the garden, too,
as you tread and travel
this broken pathway
where the sun does not dazzle

but claims company with
all these half-hidden things
and raising their gaze
does not ask of them wings—

fissures and grained dirt,
shucked shells and pebble,
a sprinkle of shatterings,
a grist of gravel

where the print and seal
the travelling foot has set
declares, Jorge Guillén,
the integrity of the planet.


## GEESE GOING SOUTH


Planing in, on the autumn gusts,
   Fleeing the inclement north, they sound
More like a hunting pack, hound
   Answering hound, than fugitives from the cold:
Flocks, skeining the air-lanes
   In stately buoyancy even seem
To dance, but one's weightless dream
   Of what they feel or are, must yield
The nearer they approach. I sense the weariness
   Of wings that bring them circling down
Onto this cut corn-field
   That offers small sustenance but rest
Among its husks and straw. Rest—
   Yet they continue calling from extended throats
As they did in flight, expending still
   Energies that they will not stint
Crying to one another—is it?—encouragement.
   I break cover for a clearer sight, but they

Instantly perceive this senseless foray
	No hunter would attempt: a thousand birds
At the snap and spread of a great fan,
	A winnowing of wings, rise up
Yelping in unison, weariness turned to power,
	And tower away to a further field
Where others are arriving. I leave them there
	On the high ridge snow will soon possess.
A moon that was rising as the birds came down
	Watches me through the trees. I too descend
Towards the firefly town lights of the valley.
	What does a goose, I ask myself,
Dream of among its kind, or are they all
	Of a single mind where moonlight shows
The flight-lanes they still strain towards
	Even in sleep? . . . In sleep
The town beside these transient neighbours
	Scarcely dreams of their nocturnal presence
Awaiting dawn, the serpentine stirrings
	And restless moon-glossed wings,
Numb at arrival, aching to be gone.


## THE STAIR


The limbs of the giant spruce that leans
	So close to the house, have formed
A kind of stair, a walk-way
	Up to the summit. The squirrel that lives here
Scorns to descend it step by step,
	But with an insane bravado runs
To a branch end, then drops
	Accurately off and, six flights down,
Arrives upright, pine-cone in hand,
	To remain there, tear at and eat it:

Perfectly secure, he is perfectly sane.
    Today, comes snow. We should accept
The long-standing invitation
    To climb those now carpeted treads,
But snow and commonsense say no—
    Such analogues are not to be acted on.
And yet we inhabit our images: squirrel
    Can even seem a god of heights,
The tree his spruce fane. The animal
    Is asleep, and if he were not, he would be
Unconscious of the place devised which we
    Take into our minds and so ascend
The real by way of the imaginary tree:
    Both lean to the house together,
And, even without their deity, can teach
    These wooden walls that this house is a tree house:
We live in a place always just out of reach.


## HACIENDA


What I like is when
men take a thing—
this river, say—
and, in the succinctest way,
use and transform it:
at the fall's head here
they have diverted
part of the flow:
a channel now
receives and passes on
through its downhill slot
all of the directed
force that is not
there in untaught nature:
the compacted stream

angles out three ways—one
turns a turbine
to refine the coffee bean;
two flows through
to a grist mill; three
concentrates into
a swirling rush to fill
the open-air Jacuzzi
of planter and family—
then, each rill
released from its man-made
duty shoots out and on
back to its bed
at the foot of the fall,
re-joining itself again to spread
under palm and plantain
across the valley floor,
once more a river.

*Puerto Rico*


## RESPONSE TO HOPKINS

*'What by your measure is the heaven of desire . . . ?'*


Camomile sweetens the cliff-top grass:
    Below, vivid uncertainties disturb
The massing of these waters: you would not think
    That the tide was receding where they beat,
As the wind piling wave on wave
    Pulls against the insistence of the moon.
And do they belong to the sea or to the sky
    These purples and these greens? The water
Washing its predilections from the eye,
    Carries such light in it, that when the hawks
Red-brown flash by, their colour
    Lightens at the reflection from beneath. Above,

All kinds of cloud—cumulus climbing,
    Fair weather dapple and horizon mist,
Fill up the air-lanes all the way
    Inland to Dartmoor. Their shadows
Move on the waste, hastening across,
    Masking each sunburst and so transform
Space to an inland sea awaiting storm.
    What by my measure is the heaven of desire?
This inconstant constancy—earth, water, fire.


## SONG

To enter the real,
how far
must we feel beyond
the world in which we already are?

It is all here
but we are not. If we could see
and hear only half
the flawed symphony,

we might cease
nervously to infer
the intentions of
an unimaginable author

and stand,
senses and tongues unbound,
in the spaces of that land
our fathers brought us to,

where, what will be well
or not well,
only time
or time's undoing can tell.

195

# SECOND SONG

On each receding bush,
the stipple of snow today
has posted into the distance
this silent company

on the alert for openings
which yesterday were not there,
tracking through field and covert
into the fullness here;

and not on bushes only,
but on stump, root, stone—
why is it a change of weather merely
finds directions where there were none?—

so that each Roman road,
on entering the maze,
crosses the hills in confusion
at the infinity of ways

only a little snow
has chalked in everywhere,
as if a whole landscape might be unrolled
out of the atmosphere.

# BEFORE THE CONCERT

If I could lay hold
on this glass of water and the stable
transparency of its contents
that contain an image of the table

on which it stands—under the glass
a draped, red cloth—
then I should possess not only
that coolness and that red, but both

of the foreshortened lutes
waiting to make music there,
under a curving window
on either side of the reflected score,

but the lutenist
(whose throat is sore today)
lowers a Brobdingnagian hand
and takes away

this universe, and I
watch it wash and disappear
over the threshold of his dryness,
until it's clear—

those minute instruments,
their world quicksilvering into water
under a melting window—
that is a room I shall never enter.

# PICKING MUSHROOMS BY MOONLIGHT

Strange how these tiny moons across the meadows,
Wax with the moon itself out of the shadows.
Harvest is over, yet this scattered crop,
Solidifying moonlight, drop by drop,
Answers to the urging of that O,
And so do we, exclaiming as we go,
With rounded lips translating shape to sound,
At finding so much treasure on the ground
Marked out by light. We stoop and gather there
These lunar fruits of the advancing year:
So late in time, yet timely at this date,
They show what forces linger and outwait
Each change of season, rhyme made visible
And felt on the fingertips at every pull.

# *Jubilation* (1995)

from 'For A Granddaughter'

## 1 ON THE TERRACE

*'Blest the infant Babe . . .'*

Four of the generations are taking tea,
Except that one of them is taking milk:
It is an English, autumnal afternoon,
The texture of the air half serge, half silk.

It is an English, autumnal afternoon,
And all four of the seasons are sitting here,
Except that one of them lies interfused
With the flesh that feeds, the arm that cradles her.

The seasons are talking in a fugue of voices,
Except that she is trying out the sounds
Through which her tongue must learn to reach the words
To speak with the world which summons and surrounds

Her kindling senses: the circumference
Of many circles draws her from her warm
Dark continuity with all things close,
To know more than the flesh, the food, the arm—

That circle within the talking circle here,
By the old house, its stone-flagged passageway,
Within the circle of the lawn, the flowers, the trees,
The young attention widening where they sway.

## 2 TO BE READ LATER ON

Poets, my dear, are much the same as you:
Watching whatever shapes come into view,
They try a murmur, a melodious sound
To suit the sense of what it is they've found
And go on finding, as they write and pause,
Their aim as much the wonder as the cause.
I watched today what would have pleased you, too—
The shadows on the curtains where they blew
In at the window, shadows that showed how
(The frame quite rigid, yet the lines one flow)
Wrought metal can turn molten in the sun
Leaping along the muslins as they run,
A whirl of lattices, a flying net,
The whole breath of the day caught up in it.
Mallarmé (a poet you must read)
Wrote of une dentelle abolie—indeed
The sun writes on a curtain and erases
(In going out) those lines that are its phrases.
Whether the conflict is a birth aborted,
A Work unconsummated he had courted
(You'll spot the allusion when you read his verse
Or hear how Boulez makes the terse more terse),
For us that flowing through the window space
Could only fill more full the blowing lace,
As if our futures—yes, both mine and yours—
Were breathed towards us off the Severn's shores,
And when you lift this poem to your ear
One day, it is that breath of ocean you will hear.

## 3 JESSICA LEARNED TO KISS

Jessica learned to kiss,
Yet never would
Kiss me. This

Withholding of a kiss
Seemed to be
Part of her glee
At parting.

Or was she
Wise enough to see
That to defer
Made time doubt
Its hold on her
And me?

At all events
Only this week,
Perhaps disenchanted
With philosophic teasing,
A kiss she planted
On my cheek.


## 6 TO MY DAUGHTER

'Families', I said, conscious that I could not find
    The adequate epithet, 'are nice.'
'Nice families', you replied, adding
    To the faded adjective a tiny spice,
'Are nice.' What I had meant was this:
    How far we (a wandering family) have come

Since that day I backpacked you down
    Into an Arizona canyon with its river
Idling below us, broad and slow;
    Next, it was the steady Susquehanna;
Now swifter currents of the Severn show
    That time is never at a stand, although the daughter
You are leading by the hand, to me
    Seems that same child cradled in Arizona.
No—you are right—: *nice* will never do:
    But it is only families can review
Time in this way—the ties of blood
    Rooting us in place, not like the unmoving trees,
And yet, as subject to earth, water, time
    As they, our stay and story linked in rhyme.


## AGAINST TRAVEL


These days are best when one goes nowhere,
The house a reservoir of quiet change,
The creak of furniture, the window panes
Brushed by the half-rhymes of activities
That do not quite declare what thing it was
Gave rise to them outside. The colours, even,
Accord with the tenor of the day—yes, 'grey'
You will hear reported of the weather,
But what a grey, in which the tinges hover,
About to catch, although they still hold back
The blaze that's in them should the sun appear,
And yet it does not. Then the window pane
With a tremor of glass acknowledges
The distant boom of a departing plane.

# TO VASKO POPA IN ROME

'Rome I dislike,' you said in French,
   'With its imperial pretensions.' You
Were the least imperious of men, in verse
   And person. We met only once again
And it was clear your days were near their end,
   Your life and death feeding on cigarette
On cigarette, 'Like a prince in exile,'
   Someone said, but that seemed fanciful for a man
Indifferent to empire. You were in exile from yourself,
   From that puzzled ebullience, watchful irony,
Balanced, it seemed almost bodily—
   For you were then a man of ample flesh—
Between Gallic precision, Italian largesse,
   As our conversation veered from tongue to tongue
In search of words adequate to express
   Our sense of the occasion. As to princeliness, I recall
Hearing you muse, 'Hughes, they say,'
   (Crossing the Borghese park near midnight)
'Lives like a prince.' 'That's true,'
   Was my reply, 'if generosity's what they intend,
And if you are his guest or friend, it's you
   Who live like one.' Pacing on,
Complaining of the melancholy great cities breed,
   As if all generosity must feed that, too,
You drew your gloom from a reserve of riches
   That soon must fail. In Rome, today,
I almost persuade myself you would agree
   That the bounty of the place exceeds pretension,
Bursting on one, as when the roar
   Of the Trevi fountain rounds the corner of its square;
And that these levels of wrought stone and water—
   Metamorphosis over an ungiving ground—
Are one more form of poetry, and we
   Guests of the imagination here. The imagination

Proposes what it does not need to prove
     And, when all's said and done, what cannot be:
Now we shall never pace this square together
     Through the Roman sunlight and the autumn air.


## VALESTRIERI

*for Astrid Donadini*

The bridal veils of the olive trees, you said,
     Seeing the white nets spread
Underneath the boughs. But these
     Slung higher to catch the crop
In its fall are the hammocks of the autumn voyage
     Into winter, swung in the after-gale
That follows the first bright cloud
     Cutting mist, bringing back sun
Into the orchards here. They have cleared the ground
     Of its brush where the nets must lie—
There is to be no waste—and all is readied
     For the slow maturing of berries still green.
But the echo of volleys through the colder air
     Bursts from the presence of huntsmen there, unseen,
Lying low claiming consummation now
     In the pattering ricochet of aim on spendthrift aim.


## DOWN FROM COLONNATA

A mist keeps pushing between the peaks
     Of the serrated mountains, like the dust
Off marble from the workings underneath:
     Down from Colonnata you can hear
The quarrymen calling through the caves
     Above the reverberation of their gear

Eating through limestone. We are moving
    And so is the sun: at each angle
Of the descending road, the low light
    Meeting our eyes, surprises them whenever
It reappears striking a more vivid white
    From the crests behind us. Down
And on: the distance flashes up at us
    The flowing mercury of the sea below
That we, passing Carrara, lose
    Until it shows once more backing the plain.
But the sun has outdistanced us already,
    And reaching the level water, dipped
Beneath it, leaving a spread sheen
    Under the final height dividing us,
And across the liquid radiance there,
    A palpitation of even, marble light.


## A RETROSPECT: 1951–91


We go down by the deserted mule-track:
    Myrtle berries and purple daisies overhang
This unused pathway of cracked stones
    The walls wind round with. It leads
Between netted olive trees and enters
    La Serra from above, down past the house
Its poet[1] was born in, that will one day—
    This is a country of inscriptions—bear
Let into its wall, a crisp-cut *lapide*.
    You could still hear his mother tongue
(His mother's tongue) if only you
    Could speak it and could call out to
That woman who descends in front of us,
    Her kindling carried on her head as when

[1] Paolo Bertolani, author of the dialect poems, *Seina*.

We first came here to streets that have withstood
    Corsair and scimitar. A poor place then,
But its stone severity hospitable
    With wine and conversation round a fire
That stung the eyes with woodsmoke. She
    That solid apparition, has disappeared
Along her alley, as we turn to cross the square,
    Into a rawness blowing off the bay
That tells how the season and the world
    Are travelling to where these forty years began
In a tumultuous autumn of seastorm, cold and rain.


from 'Portuguese Pieces'

*for Gualter and Ana Maria Cunha*

## 1 ALTO MINHO

*'Não, não é nesse lago entre rochedos . . .'*
                                            Pessoa


Bees move between the rosemary and the rose.
The oranges are waiting to be picked.
The coigns of granite by the threshing floor,
The inscription of the runic mason's mark
Ask to be clarified by the hidden sun.
(Later, it will break along the river
To show where the waters of the floodtide reached
And stained with mud the lower leaves of trees
The colour of stone, a petrine fringe reflecting
In the calm beneath . . .)
Here, bread and reality are reconciled
By the excellence of maize, the spread hunks.
We are eating honey in a granite house.

                                *Quinta do Baganheiro*

## 2 PONTE DE LIMA

Lima was *limes*, limit—
beyond the river, only the mountains.
On its bank, the alameda of tall plane trees, now,
and ghostly washing
that catches the final light, the flow
of still-warm air. The blade
of the river is broken
by the housetops and the trunks
that rise between the eye and it
on the brink of the unimaginable,
its sinuosities unclear.
Was it *limes* or *limen*, limit or threshold?
They called it Lethe, the Romans, and bridged it.
Their bridge is still here.

## 3 SOAJO

A glitter of particles
embedded in bedrock—
no asphalt here: a jigsaw of granite
paves the village square.
Granite curves the well-kerb,
granite guards the grain:
from a dais of staddlestones
looms a mausoleum for maize
that rings the hill-top
with tombs for a dynasty of kings.

## 4 SWALLOWS

Swallows outshout
the turbulent street:
swallows are messengers
where the day and night meet,
bringing news
from gods older than those
who pose in the gold interiors,
on the tiled cloister wall;
and a swallow it was
that arrowed past
threatening to graze you,
but delivered itself instead,
disappeared into
the dark slot above
a lintelled doorhead.

## 6 IN LISBON

At the Versailles
The waiter talks of his pride in the place,
With its ornate soffits, mirrors, glistening wood.
Once, he had gone to look upon the face
Of the real Versailles
To see how the two compared, and found
The ceilings in the apartments of the Pompadour
Were just like these ... Pessoa, all around,
Demolitions are dragging your city down,
And cranes constructing the blank bank architecture
The future will know us by. At the Versailles
We reconsider the Pompadour and find
Only by style will you engage the affections of the mind.

# ZIPANGU

*for Yoshiko Asano*

## 1 THE PINES AT HAKONE

The pine trees will not converse with foreigners. Their aim
is to hide everything that lies beneath their crisp, dense foliage
or at their feet—those ferns, for instance, that reproduce
the pine pattern on every leaf and lie low
the air scarcely stirring them. They have learned
to keep secrets by studying the tall trunks that surround them
and that might still be living in the Edo period.
Touched by the breeze, they rock on their pliant roots
and shift slightly their green vestments, beginning to oscillate,
to lean from side to side, even to bow —
though not deeply as is customary with this people —,
as if good manners were all they had on their minds
and they had spent a long time considering the question
without coming to any conclusion. The tiny agitations of the wood
are on the surface only, and they soon resolve themselves
into the general unison of branches, heaving, subsiding.
Today the clouds are as secretive as those branches
and they refuse to reveal the summit or the sides
of Fujiyama. You sense it there, but you cannot see
its bulk or its snow-streaks that Japanese art
has made so famous. (Hiroshige was here
but on a clearer morning.) Days later
and back in the capital, I watch the carp
in the pond of the Yasukuni shrine. These fish
in their extrovert muscularity, their passion for food
are all the trees are not; they steer themselves unerringly
with a blunt muscular force, their whiskered circular mouths
forming the O which means *give*, rolling over
on one another's backs, to get what is given, and arriving
with the massive bodily impetus
of legless sumo wrestlers ruddered by flickering tails.

But this is a military shrine, its gate a tall ideogram
topped by a bar like a gigantic gun-barrel
and the mere good manners of trees do not serve here
to distract the visitor from what he wishes to understand.
Though when he rises to go, the lit lanterns,
as if disguise were after all the mark of this nation,
throw through the branches a light of festivity, a carnival glow,
their object solely to beautify the spot
and make us forget what stern ghosts linger here.


## 2 HERON


The river crosses the city over a series of falls:
at each of the falls, waiting for fish
a small white heron—sometimes
a whole group of them, all
at a respectful distance from one another.
Perhaps they have fished the river too long—
they seldom visibly produce anything from it.
Perhaps their decorative tininess is the result
merely of malnutrition. They are indifferent to traffic
flowing by on either side, and to strollers
who pause to see what they might catch.
They watch the water with such an exemplary patience,
they seem to be leftovers from a time
when the world was filled with moral admonitions
and everything had been put there to mean something.
We, however, fail to take the lesson to heart
and continue to worry over their inadequate diet.
As evening arrives, the light on the buildings
goes golden, an Italian light, and the mountains

darken and press forward to stand protectively
round the city. Midnight
and below the roadway, in the glare of passing cars,
huddle the heron, roosting with one leg raised, and bent
even in sleep, towards the flash, the fish, the disappointment.

*Kyoto*

## 3 SHUGAKUIN GARDEN

The variegated tremor
of the reflected foliage
brings autumn to the ponds:

the rising fish
create circles within circles,
pools within pools:

under garden branches
there is every sort of water
to be seen and listened to

as it talks its way downhill
through the leat of its channel
out into the rice beyond:

you will find no frontier
between the garden and the field,
between utility and beauty here.

# 4 YAMADERA

You go by the local line:
schoolchildren keep getting off the train,
returning to those villages
beneath vertical mountains.
Kumagane: conical hills
beyond the little station;
Sakunami: the sky is darkening
and so are the trees;
it will rain soon—in time
for our arrival
by this narrow way
to the deep north,
though 'deep', they say,
is a mistranslation
of the title of Bashō's book,[1]
and 'far' would be more accurate
'though less poetic,' they add.
The river in the ravine,
this intimate progress between sheer slopes,
what must it have been
for a traveller
on foot and horse-back?
Our rail-track way
is a smooth ascent
through turning maples
into cooling autumn air,
*the faint aroma of snow in it.*
It was here he wrote—
but would not write today—
*the shriek of the cicada*
*penetrates*

---

[1] The title of Bashō's travel book, *The Narrow Way to the Deep North*,
is the translation (or invention) of Nobuyuki Yuasa (Penguin Books,
1965).

*the heart of the rock.*
He came, then, in heat.
The climb up the mountain face
which is the temple
must have cost him sweat,
his feet on the thousand steps
that lead past the door of each shrine
up to the look-out where
you can take in the entire valley,
echoing, this afternoon,
with shot on shot
from a whole army
of automatic scarecrows.
The rain arrives, but does not stay,
from a grey cloud
darkening half the sky
and disappearing. On the way down
we see once again
what arrested our upward climb —
stones to the miscarried,
and prayer-wheels
to wish the unborn
a reincarnation in a human form.
And so we depart
in the light that saw his arrival —
that of late afternoon,
to wait for the train
in this still distant corner. Clearly
the poetry of 'deep'
is more accurate
than mere accuracy —
a journey to the interior
is what it must have felt like then.
They say he came as a spy
(the villages are passing in reverse order now),
that there was more to it than met the eye,
calling on abbots and warriors,
to sniff out plots before they occurred.

There is no doubt, some say,
others that it is absurd
to speculate now. And so
we leave Bashō to disappear,
deeper and deeper,
while we cross the angular paddies
towards the shapeless cities,
the mountains already drawing apart
on either side of the wide plain
into two great parallels
echoing the track of our train,
our own narrow way south.


## 5 EPILOGUE


This advanced frontier
of Asia, this chain
of volcanoes, arcadian,
alpine, weird,
its ravines noisy with waterfalls,
its countless rivers
too impetuous for navigation,
ports few and coast foam-fringed—
the tree-fern, bamboo,
banana and palm grow here
side by side
with pine, oak, beech and conifer.
Wild animals are not numerous
and no true wolf exists
(the domestic dog
is wolf-like but ill-conditioned).
The lobster stands for longevity
and all history before 500
must be classed as legendary.
This is the place

Marco Polo never visited
but, jailed by the Genovese,
rehearsed its wonders
in bad French
to a Pisan fellow prisoner
calling it
Zipangu.


## SNAPSHOT

*for Yoshikazu Uehata*

Your camera
has caught it all, the lit
angle where ceiling and wall
create their corner, the flame
in the grate, the light
down the window frame
and along the hair
of the girl seated there, her face
not quite in focus—that
is as it should be, too,
for, once seen, Eden
is in flight from you, and yet
you have set it down complete
with the asymmetries
of journal, cushion, cup,
all we might then have missed
in that gone moment when
we were living it.

# JUBILACIÓN[1]

*a letter to Juan Malpartida*

You ask me what I'm doing, now I'm free—
Books, music and our garden occupy me.
All these pursuits I share (with whom you know)
For Eden always was a place for two.
But nothing is more boring than to hear
Of someone's paradise when you're not there.
Let me assure you, robbers, rain and rot
Are of a trinity that haunt this spot
So far from town, so close to naked nature,
Both vegetable and the human creature.
Having said that, now let me give a sample
Of how we make short northern days more ample.
We rise at dawn, breakfast, then walk a mile,
Greeting the early poachers with a smile
(For what is poetry itself but poaching—
Lying in wait to see what game will spring?)
Once back, we turn to music and we play
The two-piano version of some ballet,
*Sacre du Printemps* or Debussy's *Faune*,
On what we used to call the gramophone,
To keep the active blood still briskly moving
Until we go from dancing to improving
The muscles of the mind—'in different voices'
Reading a stretch of Proust, a tale of Joyce's.
And so to verse. Today, the game lies low,
And Brenda, passing, pauses at the window,
Raps on the pane, beckons me outside. She
Thinks, though we can't plant yet, we still can tidy,
Clear the detritus from the frosty ground
With freezing fingers, and construct a mound
Of weeds and wood, then coax it to a red
And roaring blaze—potash for each bed,

[1] The Spanish for retirement.

As Virgil of *The Georgics* might have said.
I signal back my depth of inspiration,
The piece I'm finishing for *Poetry Nation*
(What nation, as a nation, ever cared
A bad peseta or a dry goose turd
For poetry?) Our Shelley's right, of course,
You can't spur on a spavined Pegasus
Or, as he puts it, 'There's no man can say
I must, I will, I shall write poetry.'—
Or he can say it and no verse appear.
As you now see (or would if you were here)
The winter sunlight sends its invitation
To shelve these mysteries of inspiration
And breathe the air—daybreak at noon, it seems,
The swift de-misting of these British beams
(Our watercolour school was full of such
Transient effects—we took them from the Dutch).
Strange how this wooded valley, like a book
Open beneath the light, repays your look
With sentences, whole passages and pages
Where space, not words, 's the medium that assuages
The thirsty eye, syntactically solid,
Unlike the smog-smudged acres of Madrid
Boiling in sun and oil. You must excuse
These loose effusions of the patriot muse.
Not everybody's smitten with this spot—
When Chatwin lived here, he declared he was not,
His cool, blue eye alighting only on
Far distant vistas Patagonian,
Untrammelled in the ties of local life,
Lost to the county, to both friends and wife.
We'd walk together, talking distant parts—
He thought we all were nomads in our hearts.
Perhaps we are, but I prefer to go
And to return, a company of two.
Hence jubilation at my *jubilación*
That we, together, leave behind our *nación*
And visit yours—or, just look up, you'll see

The vapour trails above us, westerly
The high direction of their subtle line,
Spun between Severn and Hudson, and a sign
That we shall soon be passing at that height
And, if the weather's clear, catch our last sight
Of Gloucestershire beneath us as we go.
But I must use 'la pelle et le râteau'
(Things that were images for Baudelaire),
And with the backache, spade and rake, prepare
The soil to plant our crops in on returning.
So I must pause from versing and start burning,
To anticipate the time we're once more here
In the great cycle of the ceaseless year.


## THE TRACK OF THE DEER


             ... The track of the deer
That strayed last night into the garden,
Stops beneath the fruitless apple tree,
Shaped out and shimmering with that frost
You can feel here at the edge of all imaginings:
The departed deer glimmers with the presence
Of sensed, substantial and yet absent things.


## THE SHADOW


The sun flung out at the foot of the tree
A perfect shadow on snow: we found that we
Were suddenly walking through this replica,
The arteries of this map of winter
Offering a hundred pathways up the hill
Too intricate to follow. We stood still

Among the complications of summit branches
Of a mid-field tree far from all other trees.
Or was it roots were opening through the white
An underworld thoroughfare towards daylight?
There stretched the silence of that dark frontier,
Ignoring the stir of the branches where
A wind was disturbing their quiet and
Rippled the floating shadow without sound
Like a current from beneath, as we strode through
And on into a world of untrodden snow,
The shadow all at once gone out as the sun withdrew.


# WALKS


The walks of our age
are like the walks of our youth:
we turned then page on page
of a legible half-truth

where what was written
was trees, contours, pathways—
and what arose as we read them
half conversation, half praise—

and the canals, walls, fields
outside of the town
extended geographies
that were and were not our own

to the foot of the rocks
whose naked strata threw
their stone gaze down at us—
a look that we could not look through.


219

That gaze is on us now:
a more relenting scene
returns our words to us,
tells us that what we mean

cannot contain
half the dazzle and height
surrounding us here:
words put to flight,

the silence outweighs them
yet still leans to this page
to overhear what we talk of
in the walks of our age.

## A DOGGEREL FOR MY SEVENTIETH BIRTHDAY

*to my wife*

I see now all the things I shall not do—
Read the whole of *À la Recherche* to you,
Learn Greek enough to tackle Sophocles
No longer fog-bound in translatorese.
It's difficult enough to keep in trim
Italian, stop French from going dim,
See that my German doesn't wholly vanish,
Or speaking Tuscan strangulate my Spanish.
So, Sophocles, farewell. I still can pace
On uncertain feet the labyrinths of Horace—
Helped by that crib of Smart's that I once found,
Dusted and bought for far less than one pound.
That was before all selling became dealing
And profit just another word for stealing.
Go south, young man! Yet now I'm far too old
To join the other poets in that fold
Where puffs and prizes 're handled by a clique
Who haunt each other's parties week by week.
Now critics will grow kinder to my verse,
Since they can see the shadow of the hearse
Creeping across my pages. Youth, farewell,
Though not without that retrospective swell
Stretching the sails of age's caravel.
Happy those early days when we supposed
Verse either good or bad, the same as prose.
What culpable innocence, for now we see
The point is poetry's unreadability

Where unintentions couple and produce
Meanings unmeant and monsters on the loose
Less rational than that of Frankenstein
Who wished to be understood. That wish is mine.
I lived for art, as Tosca says, harmed none,
Suffered to see harms casually done;
I lived for you and friendship, made my verse
Out of that daily mutual universe
Surrounding us whichever way we look,
A plenitude to overflow each book.
And so my birthday, brief day, 's come and gone:
What solemn music shall we play it out on?
Not *Götterdämmerung*—the gods have died
But we remain, so why not take the tide
With Nielsen's *Inextinguishable*? I think
The January sun about to sink
Is all the *Untergang* we need tonight.
Short as the day is, yet a lingering light
Tells us the shortest day of all has been,
And leaves us now this dubious in-between,
While the year prepares to make itself anew,
As chrysalises, trees and poets do.


## A BACKWARD GLANCE


Searching my verse, to read what I'd once said,
It was the names on names of friends I read
And yours in every book, that made me see
How love and friendship nurture poetry.